Contents

GENERAL INSTRUCTIONS

FOAM TO STONE

Transforming lightweight STYROFOAM* brand foam into "faux stone" involves four basic steps that anyone can master with ease. Follow these steps for all 16 projects in the book.

Step 1: Prepare the form by cutting and assembling the styrofoam pieces.

Step 2: Cover the form with a thin layer of papier-mâché, to give it a smooth surface.

Step 3: Use modeling paste to add stone-like textures and raised relief accents.

Step 4: Paint and antique. Use gold leaf or crackled effects to add a special touch to individual projects.

*Trademark of The Dow Chemical Co.

1 CONSTRUCT

2 PAPIER MÂCHÉ

3 MODEL/EMBELLISH

4 PAINT

MATERIALS

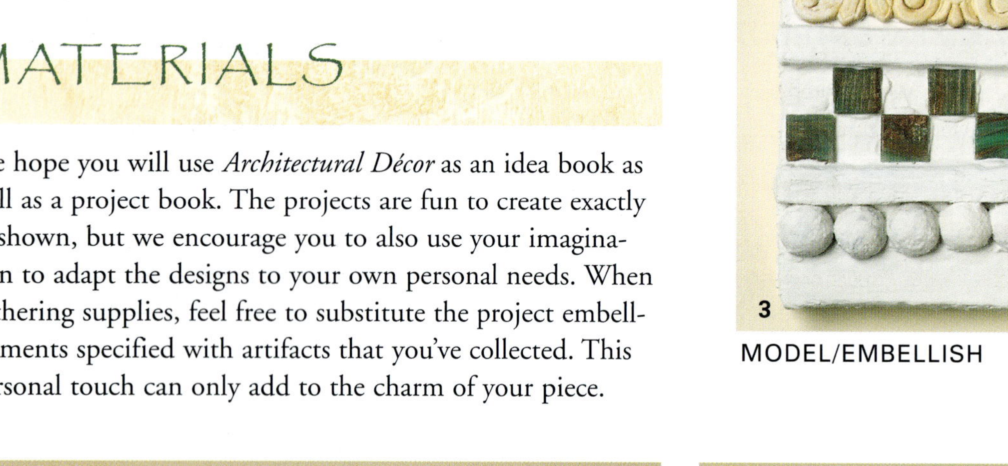

We hope you will use *Architectural Décor* as an idea book as well as a project book. The projects are fun to create exactly as shown, but we encourage you to also use your imagination to adapt the designs to your own personal needs. When gathering supplies, feel free to substitute the project embellishments specified with artifacts that you've collected. This personal touch can only add to the charm of your piece.

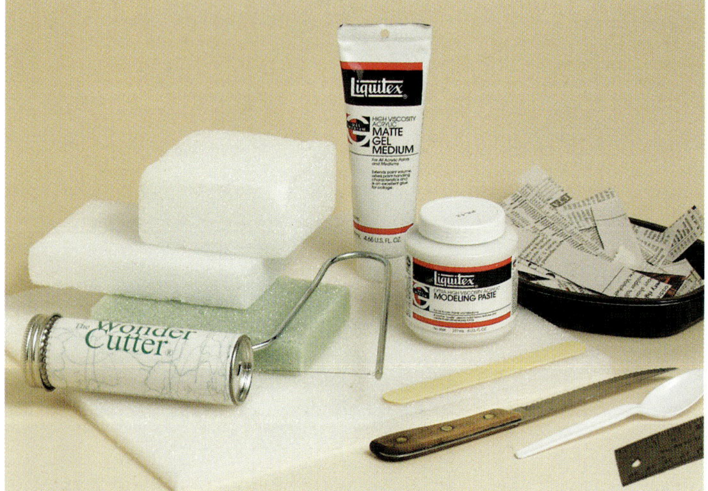

Building and Modeling Supplies (left to right): back row, *styrofoam, Liquitex Matte Gel Medium, Liquitex Modeling Paste, newspaper strips in disposable plastic container for papier-mâché;* ***front row,*** *Wonder Cutter (optional), craft stick, serrated knife, plastic spoon, ruler.*

Painting Supplies (left to right): back row, *DecoArt Multi-Purpose Sealer, water container, paper plate;* ***middle row,*** *DecoArt Americana Acrylic Paint, DecoArt Heavenly Hues Plaster and Ceramic Wash, makeup sponge, cotton swabs;* ***front row,*** *soft cloth, Loew-Cornell brushes (#4 liner, #00 fan, #6 round, ½" and 1" wash/glaze).*

GENERAL SUPPLIES:

You may already have these general supplies on hand: pencil, fine-line permanent marking pen, scissors, tracing paper, sandpaper or sanding pad, metal ruler, and tacky glue.

MODELING SUPPLIES:

Styrofoam and Cutting Tools: Styrofoam is readily available in the floral department of your craft store. It comes in an assortment of shapes and sizes including ½" and 1" thick sheets (up to 12" x 36"), and 2" thick blocks (up to 12" x 36"). You'll also find styrofoam balls and disks in many sizes. It's easy to cut the styrofoam using a common serrated kitchen knife or you may want to purchase a *Wonder Cutter*, an inexpensive tool also found in the floral department. Use a disposable plastic spoon for gouging out depressions in the styrofoam.

Papier-mâché: Most crafters are familiar with supplies for papier-mâché: paste and strips of newspaper. For the projects in this book, use a mixture of one part modeling paste + one part matte gel medium + one part water for the paste. For the newspaper strips, cut 6" long pieces about 1"-1½" wide and tear up some small pieces to be used later as needed. Prepare the papier-mâché in a disposable plastic container so you won't have to worry about clean-up.

Modeling Paste: This versatile product is available in several different sizes (8 oz., 16 oz., 32 oz., and one gallon) and has a variety of uses: 1) to "glue" styrofoam pieces together when assembling the basic form; 2) to create texture; 3) to add stenciled and embedded designs. Apply modeling paste with a craft stick or your fingers. Touch up with wet cotton swabs.

Assorted Embellishments and Add-ons (left to right): back row, *Milestones Stone Stamps, Plaid Simply Stencil, letter J wood cutout, toile and tissue paper illustrations, DecoArt Perfect Crackle and Weathered Wood Mediums, Plaid Faster Plaster and mold;* ***middle row,*** *Delta Renaissance Foil Easy Leafing System, Mercantile Vitreous Glass Mosaic Tiles, Walnut Hollow Classic Dimensions;* ***front row,*** *seashells, beach glass, sand, Kreative Foam ornaments.*

PAINTING SUPPLIES:

Paints: Use *DecoArt Americana Acrylics* for basic painting. Use *DecoArt Heavenly Hues Plaster and Ceramic Washes* for antiquing and color accents. Use brushes and a stencil sponge or makeup sponge for dabbing on color. A paper plate works well as a painting palette. Have a water container available for cleaning brushes.

Brushes: For most projects you will need only a ½" and 1" wash/glaze brush and a #6 round for both the modeling and painting steps. Use a #00 fan brush for sealing and painting cracks and a #4 liner for painting lettering.

Sealer: Use *DecoArt Multi-Purpose Sealer* to add a final finish.

EMBELLISHMENTS AND ADD-ONS SPECIFIC TO INDIVIDUAL PROJECTS

Different embellishments and textural effects give each project its uniqueness. Embellish with the products identified in the materials list or substitute with items from your own collection, e.g., shells, polished glass, or pieces of a broken plate.

- **Decorative Wood Cutouts:** Scrolls, medallions and other ⅛" thick embossed wood pieces from *Walnut Hollow Classic Dimensions.*
- **Embedded Letter and Number Stamps:** *Milestones Traditional Style Letter & Number Stone Stamps* for embedding lettering.
- **Foils:** *Delta Renaissance Foil Easy Leafing System* (gold, silver, bronze) for adding foil embellishments.
- **Illustrations for Decoupage:** Artwork on lightweight paper or fabric works well.
- **Kreative Foam:** Three-dimensional extra dense foam ornaments available in a variety of styles.
- **Metallic Paints:** *DecoArt Dazzling Metallics* for adding gold and silver highlights.
- **Molded Plaster Accents:** Assorted dimensional pieces made with *Plaid Faster Plaster and Molds.*
- **Mosaic Tiles:** Decorative tiles from *Mercantile Vitreous Glass Mosaic,* available in several colors at your craft store.
- **Seashells, Beach Glass, Sand:** Use seashells for making fossils and embedding. Beach glass and sand are useful for adding texture. Shells and glass are available at craft stores. Find sand at the garden center.
- **Stencils:** For applying a dimensional design using modeling paste, numerous stencils are available from *Plaid Simply Stencil* or other manufacturers. To personalize or adapt the designs to your own needs, cut your own stencil from a plastic sheet such as a cover from an inexpensive plastic school folder.
- **Weathered Wood and Crackling Mediums:** Use *DecoArt Perfect Crackle (two-step)* and *DecoArt Weathered Wood Medium* to give an antique crackled or weathered look.
- **Wood Letters:** Three-dimensional letter cut from wood available at craft and hardware stores.

BASIC TECHNIQUES

CUTTING THE STYROFOAM

BLOCKS

1 Measure the required dimension on each side of the styrofoam and mark with a pencil.

2 Score a line across the block using a metal ruler and pencil.

3 Cut with a serrated knife.

4 Thicker pieces may be cut two-thirds of the way through and then snapped apart.

1

2

3

4

NARROW STRIPS

1 Lay a metal ruler along the edge of the styrofoam, allowing for the width of strip desired, and mark as above. Cut the strip with a serrated knife using the edge of the ruler as a guide.

2 Cut as many strips as needed for the project.

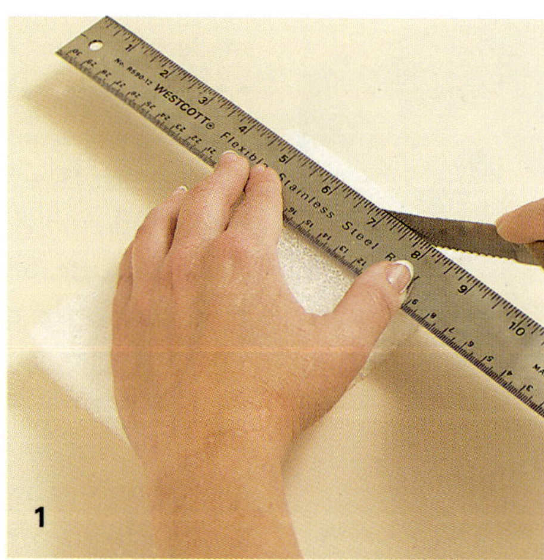

1

2

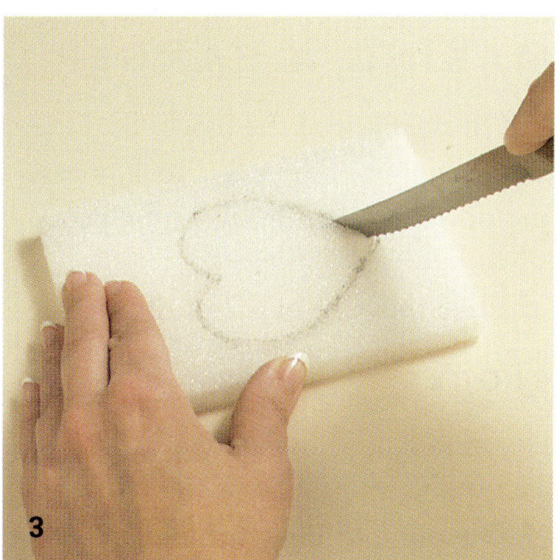

SHAPES

1 Trace the shape onto a piece of tracing paper, then lay the tracing over the styrofoam and transfer by punching holes with a pencil along the lines about ⅛" apart.

2 Score the cut line by dragging the pencil and connecting the holes.

3 Cut out the shape with a serrated knife.

SHAPING AND SMOOTHING THE EDGES

1 It is easy to shape styrofoam with your fingers. Compress using moderate pressure to round off edges or reshape areas.

2 After cutting the styrofoam, the edges may be rough. Use another piece of styrofoam like a sanding block to smooth and shape edges.

BUILDING THE STYROFOAM SHAPES:

1 Spread modeling paste on the piece to be attached.

2 Adhere to block.

MAKING A HANGER

1 On the back of the block, find the top center. For a 6" x 8" block, measure down 1½" and mark with a pencil.

2 Place the edge of a 2 oz. bottle of acrylic paint at the mark. Trace around the bottle with a pencil to make a circle, then score along your pencil line.

3 Dig out a ½" depression inside the circle using the end of a plastic spoon.

4 Shape with your fingers to smooth the edge.

1

2

3

4

COVERING WITH PAPIER-MÂCHÉ

1 Mix one part modeling paste, one part matte gel medium, and one part water. The gel medium extends the modeling paste and increases adhesion. Dip newspaper strips into the mixture, remove excess, and place onto the form. Press and smooth papier-mâché strips carefully around all shapes using a craft stick to press into place if necessary.

2 One layer of papier-mâché is enough to create a working surface.

3 On the back, papier-mâché inside the depression for the hanger. Allow papier-mâché to dry before going on to the next step.

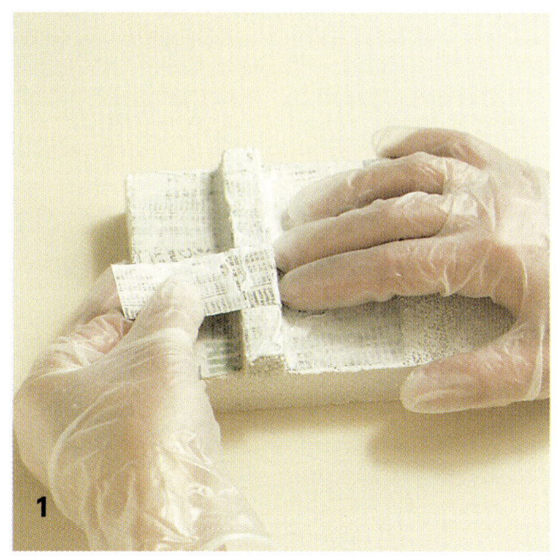
1

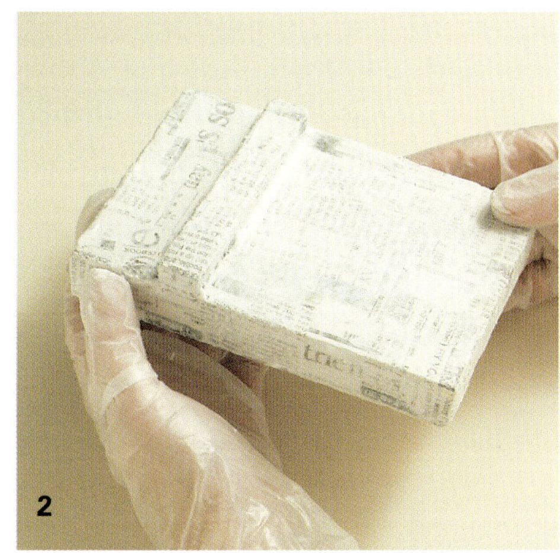
2

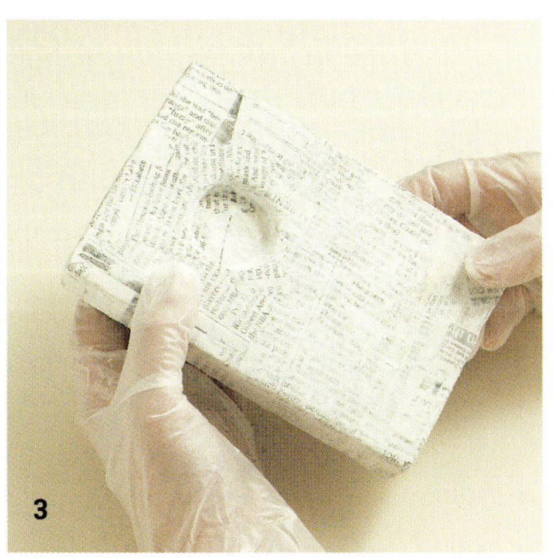
3

APPLYING THE MODELING PASTE LAYER

1 Using a brush or craft stick, apply a layer of modeling paste to create a plaster texture.

2 Smooth slightly with a wet brush, retaining some texture.

3 Be sure to extend paste onto the sides of any shapes that meet the edge of the block. This will cover edges where strips are added.

4 **Texture:** Create the rough texture on the sides of the blocks by applying a ⅛" layer of modeling paste and "pouncing" the modeling paste with your fingers or a craft stick. Add more paste if necessary. If the texture looks too rough, allow to set up slightly, then pat gently with fingers.

1

2

3

4

Architectural Modeling Tips

• If the styrofoam breaks while you are working with it, use modeling paste to glue it back together. Allow the repaired piece to dry before continuing.

• Keep brushes in water to prevent modeling paste from hardening on the bristles. Clean up hardened modeling paste with soap and warm water.

• Prepare your strips of newspaper prior to starting to papier-mâché. We used widths of paper from ½"-1½" and lengths of about 6" as well as smaller pieces for getting into tight places.

• Rough areas of modeling paste can be sanded for smoothness or reshaping.

• If the *Faster Plaster* molded pieces break, they can be repaired using tacky glue. Plaster pieces can be sanded for reshaping.

• *Heavenly Hues Plaster and Ceramic Washes* can be wiped off and reapplied many times to obtain the desired effect. Colors can be applied on top of each other when wet or dry or can be combined on the palette. Enjoy experimenting with these versatile paints.

• Commercial styrofoam cutters are available, such as the battery operated *Wonder Cutter*. They work well, but should be used with good ventilation or outdoors.

• Following the placement of the hanging hole on the back of the project, mark the top and bottom on the front of the piece to ensure the correct orientation for hanging.

• When applying a stenciled design, if the modeling paste lifts too high when you remove the stencil, lightly pat down the raised areas using a wet finger. Repair broken areas by adding more paste with the tip of a wet brush until satisfied.

CREATING CRACKS

1 When the papier-mâché and modeling paste layers are dry, create the effect of cracked/broken plaster or stone by first drawing "cracked" lines onto the surface.

2 Cut into the block with a knife, piercing through the surface into the styrofoam. Twist the knife from side to side to create wider areas of the cracks, making sure they look varied.

3 Seal the cracks by brushing modeling paste thinned with water down into the crevices using a small flat or fan brush.

CREATING A "BROKEN EDGE" EFFECT

1 Use your fingers to break off small pieces of an edge.

2 Compress the styrofoam in some places to create variety in the edge.

FOSSIL TECHNIQUE

1 Spread a ⅛" layer of modeling paste on the dry surface of the block. Allow the modeling paste to set until firm. Check by pressing gently with your finger. The surface should not be sticky.

2 Wet the object with water to prevent sticking. Impress the object into the surface, rolling gently if necessary. The example shown uses shells. Since they are rounded objects, they are rolled into the surface to leave the impression of a fossil. Allow to dry prior to painting.

ADDING EMBELLISHMENTS

1 To add embellishments such as mosaic tiles and wood pieces, first apply a 1/8" layer of modeling paste.

2 Press the embellishment into the paste.

3 Remove any excess paste on the embellishment with a wet cotton swab. Allow to dry.

4 When applying wood pieces, fill in any gaps underneath the pieces using modeling paste and a small brush. Remove excess with a wet cotton swab.

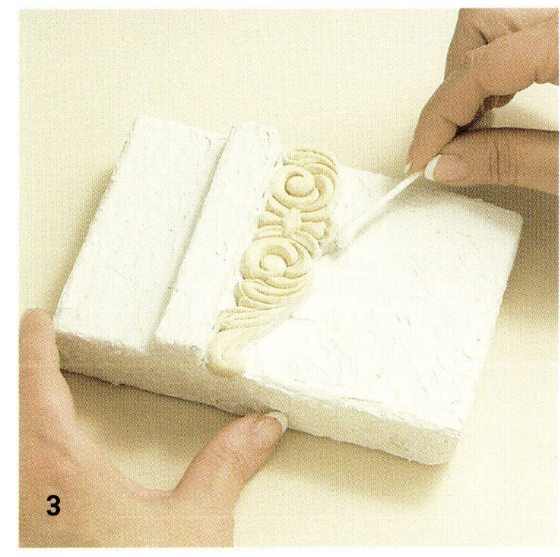

MOLDED ACCENTS

1 The molded accents used in the projects are created using *Plaid Faster Plaster* and *Plaid Faster Plaster Molds.* Follow the instructions on the bag of plaster and pour into the mold.

2 Remove the molded pieces from the mold and sand off any rough edges. If the project calls for a "broken" piece of molded plaster, use a knife to score the back of the piece where you want it to break.

3 Snap apart on the scored line.

4 Adhere the molded pieces to the surface of the block with modeling paste. Fill in areas under the edges of the molded piece with modeling paste and remove any excess with a wet cotton swab.

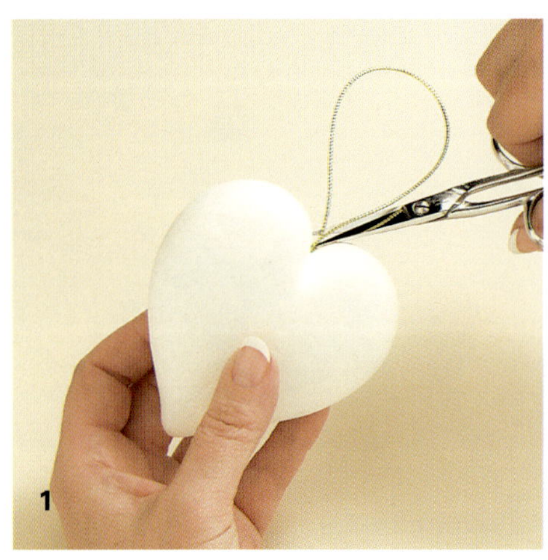

MOUNTING THREE-DIMENSIONAL FOAM SHAPES

1 If a shape has a hanger, remove it with scissors before proceeding. Some of the shapes used in the designs are rounded on both sides, yet you will need only one side for the project. Cutting the shape in half to provide a flat surface for adhering to the styrofoam is impossible when using the standard serrated knife. However, there are products on the market, such as a *Wonder Cutter* or hot knife (see Sources, page 55) that will easily cut through the foam. Be sure to use in a well-ventilated area or outdoors. Another option to cutting a shape in half is to make a depression in the block then inset the rounded form as shown in the photos 1-5 above.

2 Place the shape on top of the block in the desired position and trace around it with a pencil, scoring the styrofoam.

3 Using a knife, cut the scored line about ¼" deeper, then remove enough styrofoam to allow the rounded shape to sit halfway into the block.

4 Papier-mâché the block before adhering the shape. It is not necessary to papier-mâché inside the depression. Adhere the shape using modeling paste.

5 After placing the shape in the depression, fill around any gaps with modeling paste and smooth the edge with a wet brush.

STENCILING WITH MODELING PASTE

1 Apply a very thin layer of modeling paste to the area with your finger. This will help the stencil stick to the surface. Place the stencil on the design area and spread the modeling paste about ⅛" thick over the stencil with your fingers or a craft stick.

2 Smooth the surface of the paste with a wet brush.

(continued on next page)

3 Allow to set until the modeling paste loses its sheen. Lift the stencil gently and remove.

4 Allow to dry, then gently sand rough edges.

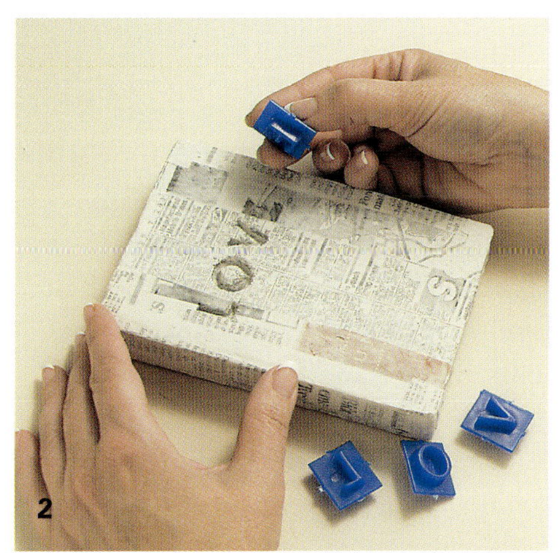

ADDING EMBOSSED LETTERING WITH STONE STAMPS

1 Apply embossed lettering to a dry papier-mâchéd surface before applying a layer of modeling paste. Trace the pattern for the lettering on tracing paper. Transfer the letters onto the surface of the block in the desired location using transfer paper and a pencil.

2 Select the stone stamp letters required for stamping. Press into the surface of the block using firm enough pressure to break through the surface and into the styrofoam. Make sure the letters are right side up. Remove stamps. Some areas may crack or be crushed, which is fine at this time.

3 Coat the surface of the entire block with a layer of modeling paste. Fill the area that has been depressed with the stone stamp letters to the level of the surface of the block. Smooth the filled area with a wet brush. The modeling paste will settle just enough so you can see where the letters have been stamped. If it is difficult to see where the depressions are, refer to your transfer drawing. Allow the filled area to set until firm to the touch (no stickiness). Depending on humidity, it should take about one hour.

4 Using the same stone stamps, press the letters into the modeling paste, one at a time, then remove gently. It is not necessary to be exactly on top of the depressed letter.

5 If the paste is raised when the stamp is removed, pat down gently with a wet finger or brush.

CLASSIC TREASURE

Nothing can be so perfect while we possess it as it will seem when remembered. —Oliver Wendell Holmes, Sr.

MATERIALS

SURFACE

2" styrofoam block, 4" x 8"
1" styrofoam disk, 8" diameter
½" styrofoam, 4" square
1½" styrofoam balls (2)

PAINTS

DecoArt Americana Acrylic Paints
Light Buttermilk
DecoArt Heavenly Hues
Earth Brown
Golden Halo
Hunter Green
Shadow Tan

BRUSHES

Loew-Cornell, Inc.
½" and 1" wash/glaze: *Series 7550*
#6 round: *Series 7000*

SUPPLIES

Liquitex Modeling Paste
Liquitex Matte Gel Medium
Printed illustration or design suitable for decoupage (we used a pear cut from *Marvel Exquisitely Elegant Tissue Wrap*)
DecoArt Perfect Crackle (two-step)
Stencil sponges or makeup sponges
Cotton swabs
Soft cloth or paper towels
DecoArt Multi-Purpose Sealer

INSTRUCTIONS

Preparation

1 Read Basic Techniques, pages 4-7.

2 On one end of the styrofoam block, create a "broken" edge. (See Special Techniques, page 8.) For the shelf, cut the 8" styrofoam disk in half and use modeling paste to adhere to the opposite end of the block as shown in the photo.

3 Using the ½" styrofoam, cut a ½" x 4" strip. Cut each of the styrofoam balls in half. Place three halves under the shelf and mark the placement for the strip. Remove the balls and adhere the strip in place with modeling paste. Papier-mâché only the rounded side of the half balls, and let dry.

4 Place a hole for hanging in the back of the block about 1¼" down from the top.

Modeling paste layer

a — Decoupage the image.

b — Brush on and wipe off antiquing colors over the entire piece.

c — Apply crackle medium. Antique Shadow Tan over crackle area.

5 Papier-mâché the entire block. Adhere ball halves using modeling paste.

6 Cut out the elements you will use for decoupage, trimming close around the edges. Set aside.

Modeling and Painting

1 Coat the entire block with a layer of modeling paste. Brush in well around balls and smooth surfaces with a soft brush dipped in water.

2 Texture the sides of the block. Lightly texture the bottom "broken" edge of the block. Allow to dry.

3 Basecoat the entire piece with Light Buttermilk. Let dry.

4 Decoupage the illustration/design on the front of the block, using matte gel medium (see figure a).

5 Brush on—then wipe off—with a soft cloth the following colors: Earth Brown, Golden Halo, Hunter Green, and Shadow Tan. Cover the entire piece, allowing very little color to remain on the image (see figure b). The shelf is predominately Shadow Tan and Golden Halo. Allow the crevices to retain color and sponge additional Hunter Green on the sides (see photo). Allow to dry.

6 Following manufacturer's instructions, apply the two-step crackle to the block front in the design area only. Rub Shadow Tan into the crackle over the front design area, and wipe off allowing color to stay in the cracks (see figure c).

Finishing

1 When dry, seal with multi-purpose sealer.

HAPPILY LOVE HEALS

One word frees us of all the weight and pain of life:
That word is love. —Sophocles

MATERIALS

SURFACE

½" styrofoam, 12" x 28"

PAINTS

DecoArt Americana Acrylic Paints
Light Buttermilk
DecoArt Heavenly Hues
Earth Brown
Shadow Tan
Soft Black
DecoArt Dazzling Metallics
Glorious Gold
Royal Ruby

BRUSHES

Loew-Cornell, Inc.
½" and 1" wash/glaze: *Series 7550*
#6 round: *Series 7000*

SUPPLIES

Tracing and transfer paper
⅛" foamcore board or heavy cardstock, 4" x 4"
Liquitex Modeling Paste
Liquitex Matte Gel Medium
Gold foil by *Delta Renaissance Easy Gold Leafing System*
Delta Renaissance Foil Adhesive
Medium-size adhesive strip (band-aid), approx. ⅝" x 2¼"
DecoArt Perfect Crackle (two-step)
Stone stamps by *Milestones Traditional Style Letter and Number Stone Stamps*
Toile image for decoupage (use napkin with toile print or scan toile fabric)
Soft cloth or paper towels
Ruler
Pin or needle
Cotton swabs
Sandpaper
Tacky glue
DecoArt Multi-Purpose Sealer

INSTRUCTIONS

Preparation

1 Read Basic Techniques, pages 4-7.

2 Cut two 12" x 12" squares from ½" styrofoam.

3 Trace the heart pattern on page 17 and transfer to ½" styrofoam. Cut out the heart shape using a serrated a knife. Smooth and shape edges using another piece of styrofoam to sand and your fingers to compress edges.

4 Measure down 1¼" from the top of one styrofoam square and create a hole for hanging. Since this will be the base square, the hole can penetrate entirely through the square. Using the other styrofoam square for the top piece, cut a 3½"-square hole in the center. Next, cut out "broken" areas as shown in the photo. (See Special Techniques, page 8.)

5 Papier-mâché each of the three shapes separately.

6 Attach the adhesive strip to a piece of ⅛" foamcore board or heavy card-stock. Cut out around the shape of the strip (see figure a, page 16). Press down on each side of the center padded area with the edge of a ruler to indent. Poke holes in this area with a pin or needle to mimic the original holes in the strip. Bend one end over as shown in the photo. Set aside.

Modeling paste layer

LOVE
HEALS

Modeling and Painting

1 Trace the words "LOVE HEALS" onto tracing paper (see pattern, page 17) and transfer to the top square using transfer paper and a pencil (see photo for placement.) Using stone stamps, press the letters into the surface, breaking through the papier-mâché layer to the styrofoam. (See Special Techniques, page 11.) Coat the top and sides of the top square with modeling paste, allowing the paste to fill the letter areas. When the paste has set up, press the letters back into their original positions.

2 Create cracks in the top piece. (See Special Techniques, page 8.)

3 Coat all sides of the base square with a layer of modeling paste and also coat the heart. Smooth the surface of the heart using a soft brush dipped in water. Coat all sides of the adhesive strip with a slightly thinner mixture of modeling paste and water, keeping the end bent and retaining the indented areas (see figure b). Smooth the surface with a soft brush dipped in water. When the adhesive strip is dry, use a pin to enlarge the holes in the center square (see figure c). Allow all pieces to dry thoroughly.

4 Basecoat the top and bottom pieces Light Buttermilk. Basecoat the heart Royal Ruby. Basecoat the adhesive strip Glorious Gold (see figure d). When dry, apply Gold foil over the adhesive strip, following manufacturer's instructions, then seal the Gold foil area (see figure e). Brush on and wipe off Soft Black on the adhesive strip (see figure f).

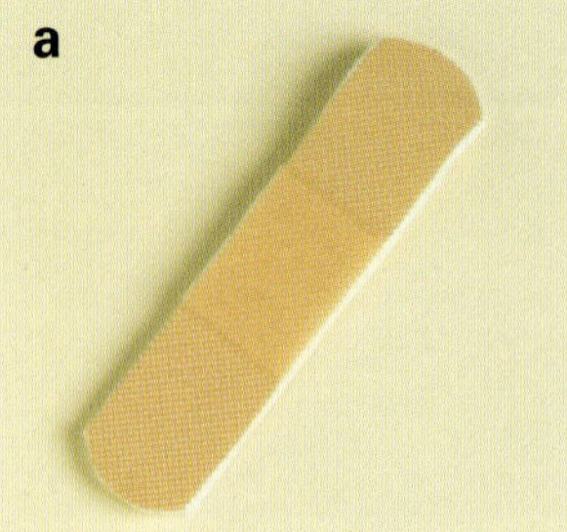

Attach band-aid to foam-core. Cut around shape.

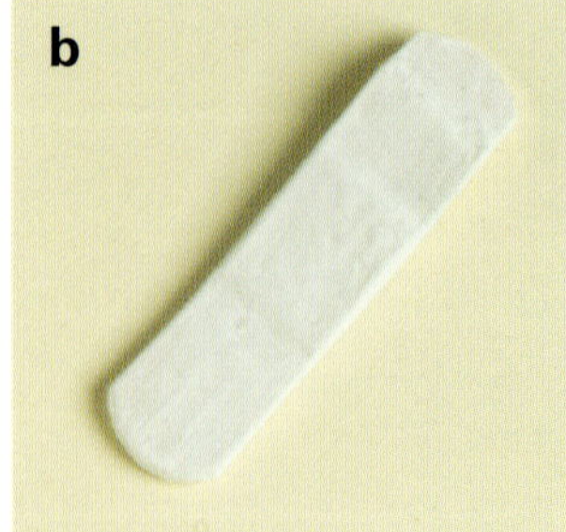

Coat with thin mixture of modeling paste.

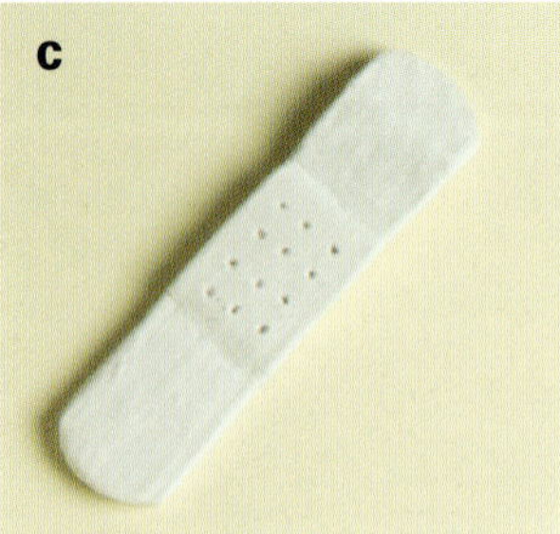

Retain indented areas and enlarge holes in center with pin.

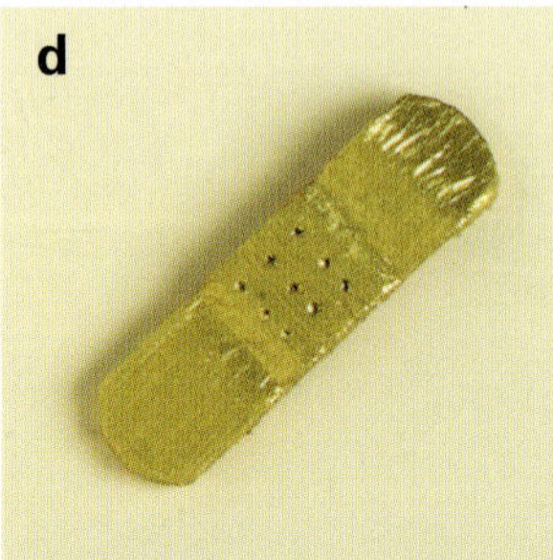

Paint Glorious Gold.

Apply Gold foil and seal.

Brush on and wipe off Soft Black.

Decoupage image.

Apply two-step crackle medium.

Antique Shadow Tan.

5 Cut the toile image to fit the bottom square and decoupage using matte gel medium (see figure g). When dry, apply crackle medium over the surface of the design, following manufacturer's instructions (see figure h). Brush Shadow Tan over the design area and wipe with a soft cloth, leaving color in the crackle texture (see figure i).

6 Brush Shadow Tan over the front of the top square; include the "broken" textured areas and sides of the square cutout. Wipe, leaving enough color to tone the lettering. Use cotton swabs to control how much color remains in the letters. Brush on and wipe off Earth Brown on the sides of the inner square and broken edges to darken.

7 Use modeling paste to attach the top and bottom layers. Smooth a layer of modeling paste to hide edges on the sides of the two layers where they meet. Wipe any excess off the top layer. Allow to dry.

8 Brush on and wipe off Shadow Tan over the sides of the block.

9 Lightly sand the front of the block, removing some paint to create a weathered look.

Finishing

1 Glue the adhesive strip to the front of the heart using tacky glue, then glue the heart in the center of the square. (See photo for placement.)

2 When thoroughly dry, seal with multi-purpose sealer.

Pattern for heart cutout

Pattern for stone stamp placement

LOVE

HEALS

PURELY INSPIRATION

Man is, above all, he who creates. And theirs alone is brotherhood who work together. —Saint-Exupery

CREATE

MATERIALS

SURFACE

1" styrofoam, 4" x 6"
½" styrofoam, 1" x 4"

PAINTS

DecoArt Americana Acrylic Paints
Burnt Umber
Lamp Black
Lt. Buttermilk
Rookwood Red
DecoArt Dazzling Metallics
Glorious Gold
DecoArt Heavenly Hues
Golden Halo
Shadow Tan
Soft Black

BRUSHES

Loew-Cornell, Inc.
½" and 1" wash/glaze: *Series 7550*
#4 liner: *Series 7350*
#6 round: *Series 7000*

SUPPLIES

Tracing and transfer paper
Liquitex Modeling Paste
Liquitex Matte Gel Medium
Decorative wood piece by *Walnut Hollow Classic Dimensions #16406*
Craft saw
Gold foil by *Delta Renaissance Foil Easy Leafing System*
Delta Renaissance Foil Adhesive
Eight mosaic tiles by *Mercantile Vitreous Glass Mosaic, Hot Molten*
Stencil sponges or makeup sponges
Sandpaper (medium)
Soft cloth or paper towels
DecoArt Multi-Purpose Sealer

INSTRUCTIONS

Preparation

1 Read Basic Techniques, pages 4-7.

2 Create a hanging hole on the back of the 4" x 6" block, approximately ¾" from the top.

3 Cut two ¼" x 4" strips from the ½" styrofoam. On the front of the block, measure down ¾" from the top and draw a horizontal line with a pencil. Using modeling paste, attach one ¼" x 4" styrofoam strip just below the line.

4 Measure up 2⅝" from the bottom, mark as before, then glue the second strip in place above the line. Let dry.

5 Papier-mâché the entire block, covering the attached strips and the inside areas of the hole on the back.

Modeling and Painting

1 Apply a layer of modeling paste to the entire block. Let dry, then texture the sides.

2 Basecoat the two ¼" strips and the back of the block with Lamp Black.

3 Use a craft saw to cut off both ends of the decorative wood piece (see photo). Sand raw edges. Spread a layer of modeling paste about ⅛" thick below the bottom bar and press the wood piece into the modeling paste. (See Special Techniques, page 9.)

4 Break one corner off four mosaic tiles. Spread a ⅛" layer of modeling paste between the two black bars and press the four whole tiles as well as the four broken tiles into the paste (broken corners should be at the edges of the block). See photo for placement. Let dry.

5 Basecoat the remaining areas of block with Lt. Buttermilk, including the wood piece and areas between tiles (see figure a, page 20). Exclude areas basecoated Lamp Black.

Modeling paste layer

CREATE
DREAM
BELIEVE

6 Brush Golden Halo over the Lt. Buttermilk basecoat. Wipe off, allowing some color to remain, particularly in the crevices. Let dry. Repeat with Shadow Tan (see figure b).

7 Brush Soft Black over the wood piece and the sides of the block. Wipe off as in last step (see figure c).

8 Dip the sponge into Glorious Gold, blot, and sponge randomly on the sides of the block. Repeat this step with Soft Black, Rookwood Red, and Lt. Buttermilk. The predominant color on the sides is Lt. Buttermilk. Change colors on the sponge at random until desired effect is achieved.

9 Foil the wood piece and the bars with Gold foil, following manufacturer's instructions. Seal and allow to dry (see figure d).

10 Brush Soft Black over the wood piece and wipe off, allowing black to remain in crevices (see figure e).

11 Using Rookwood Red, lightly brush over the wood piece and wipe off, leaving a bit of color on the top. Brush on and wipe off Lt. Buttermilk randomly over the wood piece (see figure f).

Details and Finishing

1 Trace the pattern for "CREATE" (above) onto tracing paper and transfer onto the block above the top bar, using transfer paper and pencil. Paint the letters, using the #4 liner and Burnt Umber.

2 When dry, seal the entire block with multi-purpose sealer.

CREATE

Pattern for lettering

Basecoat Lt. Buttermilk and Lamp Black.

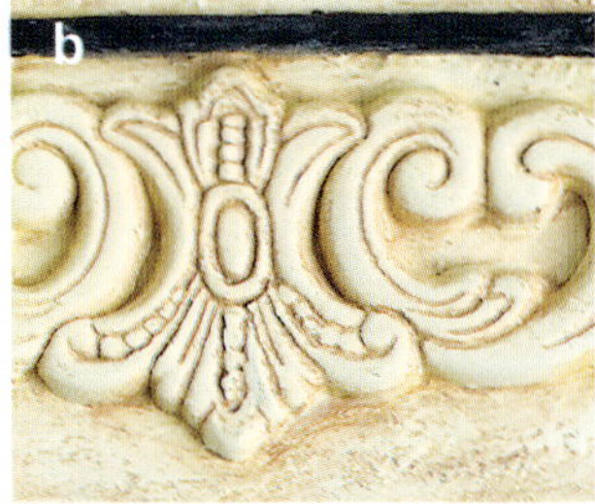

Antique with Golden Halo and Shadow Tan.

Antique wood pieces with Soft Black.

Gold foil wood and bar.

Antique over wood with Soft Black.

Antique over wood with Rookwood Red and Lt. Buttermilk.

DREAM

MATERIALS

SURFACE

1" styrofoam, 4" x 6"
½" styrofoam, 1" x 4"

PALETTE

DecoArt Americana Acrylic Paints
Lamp Black
Lt. Buttermilk
Pansy Lavender
Taupe
DecoArt Dazzling Metallics
Shimmering Silver
DecoArt Heavenly Hues
Golden Halo
Purple Heather
Soft Black

BRUSHES

Loew-Cornell, Inc.
½" and 1" wash/glaze: *Series 7550*
#4 liner: *Series 7350*
#6 round: *Series 7000*

SUPPLIES

Tracing and transfer papers
Liquitex Modeling Paste
Liquitex Matte Gel Medium
Eight mosaic tiles by *Mercantile Vitreous Glass Mosaic, Dew Metallic*
Decorative wood medallion by *Walnut Hollow Classic Dimensions #16202*

Pattern for lettering and arch

Craft saw
Sandpaper
Silver foil by *Delta Renaissance Foil Easy Leafing System*
Delta Renaissance Foil Adhesive
Stencil sponges or makeup sponges
Soft cloth or paper towels
DecoArt Multi-Purpose Sealer

INSTRUCTIONS

Preparation

1 Read Basic Techniques, pages 4-7.

2 Create a hanging hole on the back of the 4" x 6" block, approximately ¾" from the top.

3 Using the ½" styrofoam, cut two strips ⅜" x 4" and one arched piece. Trace the arch pattern (above) on tracing paper and transfer using transfer paper. On the front of the block, measure down 3⅛" from the top and draw a horizontal line with a pencil. Use modeling paste to attach one styrofoam strip just below the line. Measure ¾" up from the bottom and attach the other styrofoam strip above the line. Attach the arched styrofoam piece at the top of the block (see photo).

4 Cut the wood medallion in half using a craft saw. Sand raw edges.

5 Papier-mâché the entire block, covering the attached strips and the inside areas of the hole on the back.

Modeling and Painting

1 Apply a layer of modeling paste to the block. Allow to dry, then texture the sides.

2 Basecoat the two lower bars and

Modeling paste layer

a Basecoat Lt. Buttermilk and Lamp Black.

b Antique Golden Halo.

c Antique wood pieces with Soft Black.

d Silver foil wood and bar.

e Antique Soft Black over wood.

f Antique Purple Heather.

the back of the block Lamp Black.

3 Spread a ⅛" layer of modeling paste between the arch and the first bar and press the wood half-medallion in place.

4 Break the mosaic tiles into pieces. (Place inside a towel and tap with a hammer, using safety glasses.) Spread a ⅛" layer of modeling paste between the two lower bars and press in mosaic tiles.

5 Basecoat remaining areas of the block with Lt. Buttermilk, including the wood piece and areas between tiles (see figure a, page 21).

6 Brush on and wipe off Golden Halo over the Lt. Buttermilk, allowing color to remain in crevices (see figure b, page 21).

7 Brush on and wipe off Soft Black over the wood piece and sides of the block, allowing color to remain in crevices (see figure c, page 21).

8 Paint top and bottom areas Taupe.

9 Foil the two lower strips and wood piece with Silver foil, following manufacturer's instructions. Seal and let dry (see figure d, page 21).

10 Brush on and wipe off Soft Black over the wood piece (see figure e, page 21). Brush on and wipe off Purple Heather over the Taupe areas, the arch, and foiled areas (see figure f, page 21).

11 Dip a sponge into Taupe, blot and sponge randomly over the sides of the block. Repeat with Shimmering Silver, Purple Heather, Golden Halo and Lt. Buttermilk.

Details and Finishing

1 Trace the "DREAM" pattern on page 21 onto tracing paper and transfer to the arch, using transfer paper and pencil. Paint the letters using Pansy Lavender and the #4 liner.

2 Seal with multi-purpose sealer.

BELIEVE

MATERIALS

SURFACE

1" styrofoam, 4"x 6"
½" styrofoam, 1" x 4"

PAINTS

DecoArt Americana Acrylics
Black Green
Green Mist
Lt. Buttermilk
DecoArt Dazzling Metallics
Glorious Gold
DecoArt Heavenly Hues
Golden Halo
Patina Green
Shadow Tan
Soft Black

BRUSHES

Loew-Cornell, Inc.
½" and 1" wash/glaze: *Series 7550*
#4 liner: *Series 7350*
#6 round: *Series7000*

SUPPLIES

Tracing and transfer papers
Liquitex Modeling Paste
Liquitex Matte Gel Medium
Five mosaic tiles *by Mercantile Vitreous Glass Mosaic, Jade Metallic*
Three 1" styrofoam balls
Decorative wood piece by *Walnut Hollow Classic Dimensions #16302*
Craft saw
Copper foil by *Delta Renaissance Foil Easy Leafing System*
Delta Renaissance Foil Adhesive
Stencil sponges or makeup sponges
Soft cloth or paper towels
DecoArt Multi-Purpose Sealer

INSTRUCTIONS

Preparation

1 Read Basic Techniques, pages 4-7.

2 Create a hanging hole on the back of the 4" x 6" block, approximately ¾" from the top.

3 Using the ½" styrofoam, cut two strips ¼" x 4". Cut the three 1" styrofoam balls in half. Cut the edge of one ball in half to fit the block, if necessary.

4 On the front of the block, measure 1¼" down from the top and draw a horizontal line with a pencil. Use modeling paste to attach one ¼" x 4" styrofoam strip just below the line. Measure 2" up from the bottom of the block. Use modeling paste to attach the second styrofoam strip just above the line. Let dry.

5 Papier-mâché the entire block, covering the attached strips as well. Papier-mâché only the rounded side of five ball halves. Allow all to dry thoroughly.

Modeling and Painting

1 Apply a layer of modeling paste to the entire block. Let dry then texture the sides. Allow to dry thoroughly.

2 Using Black Green, paint the two ½" strips and back of the block. Let dry.

3 Lay the decorative wood piece on the front of the block, above the top strip. Allow one end of the wood piece to extend beyond the edge and mark to fit the block (see photo). Cut the wood at the mark using a craft saw.

4 Spread a layer of modeling paste about ⅛" thick above the top strip and press the decorative wood piece into the modeling paste. Fill in gaps under the wood and remove excess paste. (See Special Techniques, page 9.)

5 Spread a layer of modeling paste about ⅛" thick between the two strips and press in the mosaic tiles in a checkerboard pattern (see photo).

6 Using modeling paste, attach the five ball halves to the block underneath the bottom ½" strip. Fill gaps with modeling paste and remove excess paste. Dip the brush in water and

BELIEVE

Pattern for lettering

lightly brush over the flat area underneath the balls halves to smooth. Let dry thoroughly. (See Step 3, page 2, for photo of modeling layer.)

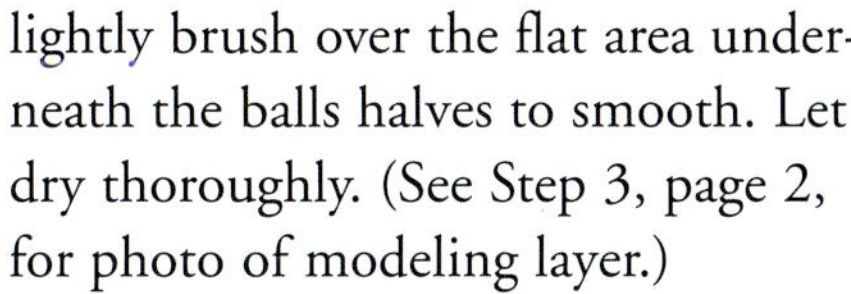

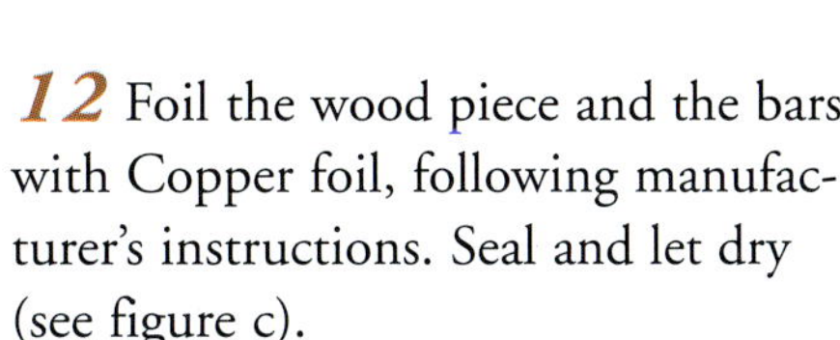

7 Basecoat remaining areas of the block with Lt. Buttermilk, including sides, decorative wood piece, and the areas between mosaic tiles. Avoid areas already basecoated with Black Green.

8 Brush Golden Halo and Shadow Tan over the Lt. Buttermilk basecoat. Wipe off with a soft cloth, allowing some color to remain, particularly in the crevices (see figure a).

9 Brush Soft Black over the wood piece (see figure b), around and between the ball halves and over the sides of the block. Wipe off as in last step.

10 Paint the area under the ball halves Patina Green.

11 Dip the sponge into Green Mist; blot and sponge randomly on sides of the block. Repeat this step with Glorious Gold, Lt. Buttermilk, Soft Black and Patina Green. Change colors on the sponge at random until desired effect is achieved.

12 Foil the wood piece and the bars with Copper foil, following manufacturer's instructions. Seal and let dry (see figure c).

13 Brush Soft Black over the wood piece and wipe off, allowing black to remain in crevices (see figure d).

14 Using Green Mist, lightly brush random strokes on the wood piece (see figure e), bars, and ball halves. Repeat using Lt. Buttermilk and Glorious Gold (see figure f).

Details and Finishing

1 Trace the "BELIEVE" pattern (above left) onto tracing paper and transfer onto the block under the ball halves, using transfer paper and pencil. Paint the letters using the #4 liner and a mixture of Black Green + Green Mist (1:1).

2 When the block is dry, seal the entire block with multi-purpose sealer.

Antique Shadow Tan.

Antique Soft Black over wood.

Copper foil wood piece and bars.

Antique Soft Black over wood piece.

Lightly brush random strokes of Green Mist.

Repeat using Lt. Buttermilk and Glorious Gold.

SEASIDE MEMORIES

Consider the sea's listless chime: Time's self it is, made audible. —Dante Gabriel Rossetti

MATERIALS

SURFACE

½" styrofoam, 12" x 28" piece

PAINTS

DecoArt Americana Acrylic Paints
Lt. Buttermilk
Soft Peach
DecoArt Heavenly Hues
Earth Brown
Golden Halo
Sea Spray
Shadow Tan

BRUSHES

Loew-Cornell, Inc.
½" and 1" wash/glaze: *Series 7550*
#6 round: *Series 7000*

SUPPLIES

Liquitex Modeling Paste
Liquitex Matte Gel Medium
Foam scallop shell (2⅜" x 2⅜") by *Kreative Foam* (or use an actual shell from own collection about the same size)
Wonder Cutter (optional)
Assorted small seashells, one package (purchased at local craft store, or use shells from your own collection)
Tumbled beach glass, one package
½ cup of coarse play sand (available at local landscape supply)
Tacky glue
Soft cloth or paper towels
Cotton swabs
DecoArt Americana Spray Sealer/Finisher

INSTRUCTIONS

Preparation

1 Read Basic Techniques, pages 4-7.

2 Cut two 12" x 12" squares from ½" styrofoam.

3 Measure down 1¼" from the top of one styrofoam square and create a hole for hanging. Since this will be the base square, the hanging hole can penetrate entirely through the square. Cut a 3½" x 3½" square hole in the center of the other styrofoam square. Break off opposite corners, creating "broken" edges. (See photo for placement of broken edges and Special Techniques, page 8.) This will be the top square.

4 Cut a 3½" x 3½" square from the remaining styrofoam and compress edges with fingers to make uneven. If you choose to use a foam scallop shell, cut it in half using a *Wonder Cutter* (see tips, page 7) or make a depression in the square deep enough to accommodate half of the foam shape. (See Special Techniques, page 10.) Set aside.

5 Papier-mâché all three shapes separately. Inset the foam shell into the small square or adhere an actual shell using modeling paste.

Modeling and Painting

1 Attach the top square to the base using modeling paste.

2 Coat the entire block with a layer of modeling paste. Smooth a layer of modeling paste to hide edges on the side of the two layers where they meet. Wipe off excess.

3 Coat the front and sides of the small square with modeling paste. Bring the paste up to the edge of the shell and smooth with a soft brush dipped in water.

4 Basecoat the main block Lt. Buttermilk. Add another layer of modeling paste about ⅛" thick to the front of the block (smoothing and feathering it out to the edges) and embed a number of small shells (eight used in

Modeling paste layer

model) and a few pieces of beach glass into the modeling paste. (See photo above.)

5 When the modeling paste sets up, use a variety of small shells to create a fossil pattern. (Refer to the photo for placement and Special Techniques, page 8, for making fossils.) Sprinkle a bit of sand across the front if desired.

6 Brush on Earth Brown inside the center square on the main block and continue the color up the sides of this inner square, then wipe off with a soft cloth. Next, brush on and wipe off Sea Spray over the Earth Brown just on the sides. Allow these areas to remain dark.

7 Brush on and wipe off Golden Halo over the entire block, avoiding the embedded shells and beach glass (see figure a). Repeat with Shadow Tan. Allow more color to stay in the fossil areas (see figure b). Using Lt. Buttermilk, brush across the raised portions of the fossil areas to highlight (see figure c).

8 Paint the large shell Soft Peach then lightly wipe the raised scallop areas. On the front and sides of the small square, brush on and wipe off Earth Brown (see figure d). Brush on and wipe off Sea Spray on the sides only (see figure e).When dry, lightly brush Light Buttermilk on the shell to highlight the raised scallop areas (see figure f).

9 Spread a thick layer of matte gel medium in the two corners on the base square next to the broken edges (see photo). Press a selection of beach glass and shells into the areas, leaving some exposed spaces for the coarse sand. Sprinkle sand over the areas and press gently into the matte gel medium with your fingers. Use a brush to sweep sand into place and to remove excess sand. Allow to dry. If necessary, add more matte gel medium in any bare or thin areas and repeat the application of the sand. The matte gel medium will dry clear.

Finishing

1 Glue the small square into place in the center of the block using tacky glue.

2 Seal with spray sealer/finisher. (The sealer needs to be applied by a spray method because of the sandy areas.)

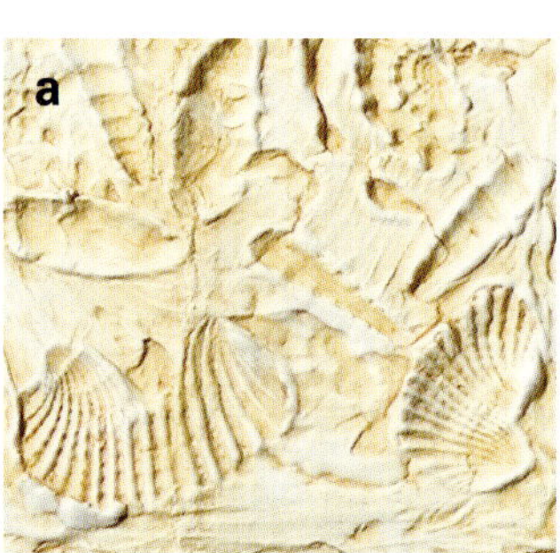

a

Antique Golden Halo.

b

Antique Shadow Tan.

c

Highlight raised fossil areas with Lt. Buttermilk.

d

Basecoat shell Soft Peach. Antique small square Earth Brown.

e

Antique sides of small square with Sea Spray.

f

Lightly brush Lt. Buttermilk over raised scallop areas.

Patterns for

HEART IN HAND

Instructions on page 34

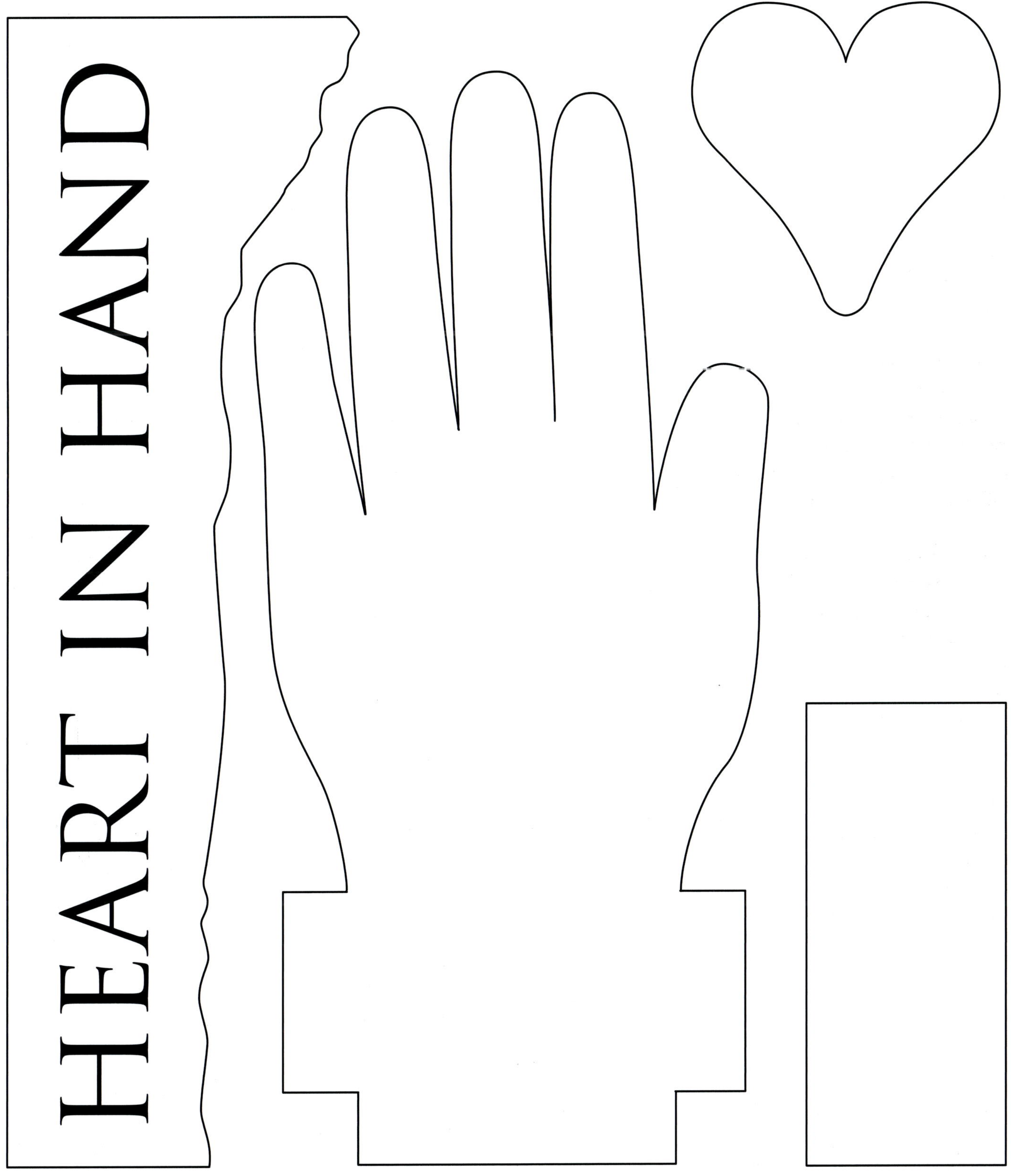

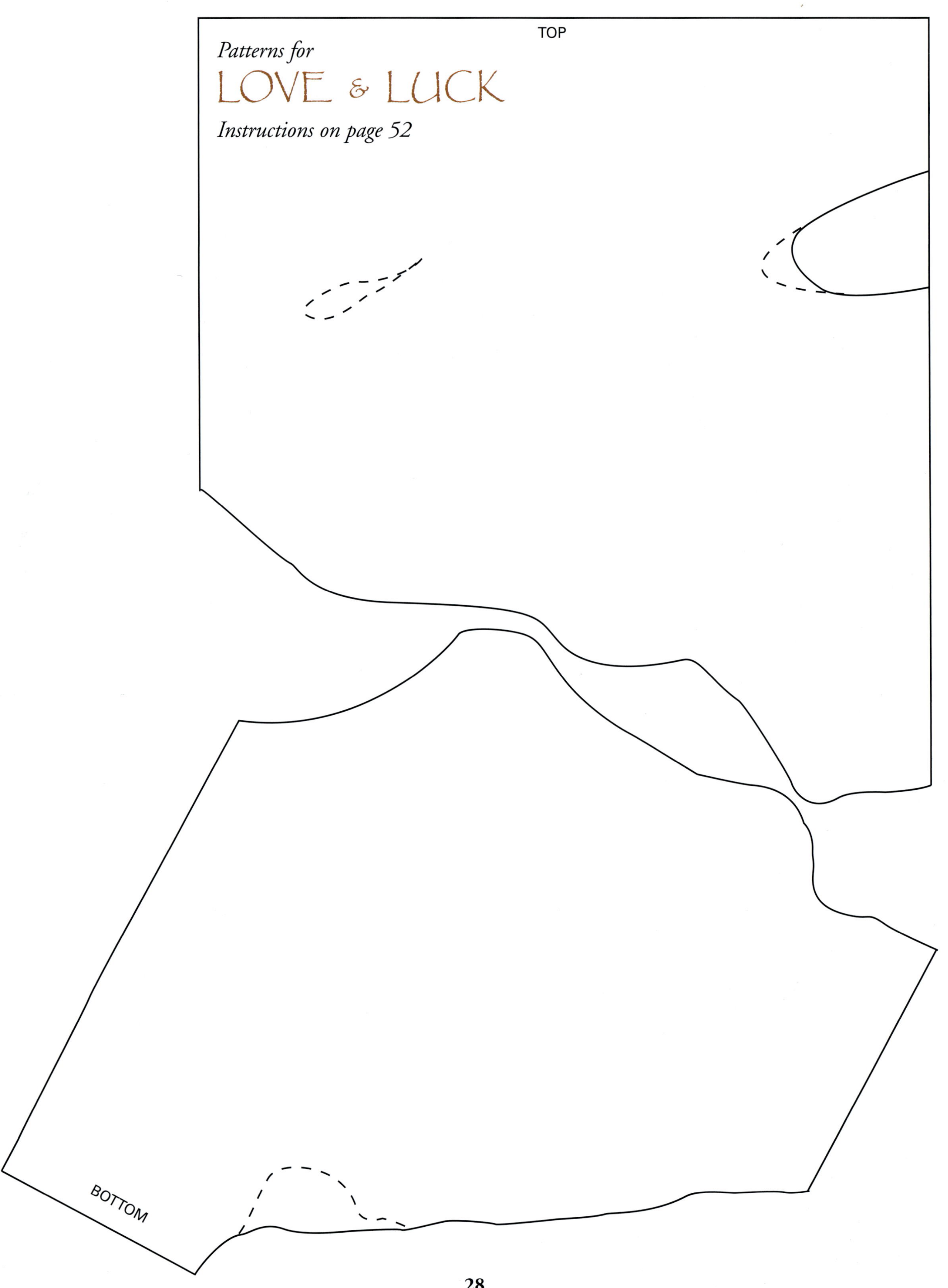
TOP
Patterns for
LOVE & LUCK
Instructions on page 52
BOTTOM

Pattern for

NATURAL REFLECTIONS

Instructions on pages 44

LESSONS FROM THE HEART

It is only with the heart that one can see rightly; what is essential is invisible to the eye. —Saint-Exupéry

FLEUR-DE-LIS

MATERIALS

SURFACE

1" styrofoam, 6" x 8"
½" styrofoam, 6" x 12"

PAINTS

DecoArt Americana Acrylic Paints
Buttermilk
Lamp Black
Lt. Buttermilk
Rookwood Red
DecoArt Heavenly Hues
Earth Brown
Golden Halo
Shadow Tan
Soft Black
DecoArt Dazzling Metallics
Glorious Gold

BRUSHES

Loew-Cornell, Inc.
½" and 1" wash/glaze: *Series 7550*
#6 round: *Series 7000*
#00 fan: *Series 7200*

SUPPLIES

Liquitex Modeling Paste
Liquitex Matte Gel Medium
Fleur-de-lis foam shape (4" x 3¼") by *Kreative Foam*
Decorative wood piece by *Walnut Hollow Classic Dimensions #16509*
Stencil by *Plaid Simply Stencil Fruit Medley #281367*
DecoArt Weathered Wood Crackling Medium
Soft cloth or paper towels
Cotton swabs
Stencil sponges or makeup sponges
Craft saw
Sandpaper (fine)
DecoArt Multi-Purpose Sealer

INSTRUCTIONS

Preparation

1 Read Basic Techniques, pages 4-7.

2 Cut three pieces from the ½" styrofoam: 6" x 8", 1¼" x 6" and ½" x 6".

3 Attach the 6" x 8" piece of ½" styrofoam to the 6" x 8" block of 1" styrofoam. Create a hanging hole for the back approximately 1½" down from the center top.

4 On the front of the block, attach the 1¼" x 6" styrofoam piece at the top edge, then glue the ½" x 6" bar on top of the larger piece, positioning it at the top edge (see photos).

5 Cut the decorative wood piece using a craft saw. Refer to the illustration on page 32 for the cutting lines. Sand the raw edges with sandpaper.

6 Cut the fleur-de-lis foam shape in half with a *Wonder Cutter* (see tips, page 7), or create a depression in the block deep enough to accommodate half of the shape. (See Special Techniques, page 10.) Center the fleur-de-lis just underneath the 1¼" top bar.

7 Before attaching the fleur-de-lis, papier-mâché the main block. If you choose to make a depression for the foam shape, there is no need to papier-mâché inside.

Modeling and Painting

1 After papier-mâché is dry, adhere the fleur-de-lis using modeling paste.

2 Coat the block with a layer of modeling paste. Bring the modeling paste up to the edge of the fleur-de-lis, smoothing with a wet brush to make a smooth transition. Texture the sides of the block.

3 Spread a ⅛" layer of modeling paste in areas where the decorative wood sections will be placed (see photo). Press wood pieces into the modeling paste. Fill gaps under edges if necessary. (See Special Techniques, page 9.)

4 Using modeling paste, stencil the border pattern along the top edge of the block. (See Special Techniques, page 10.) Let dry thoroughly. Sand edges lightly with sandpaper, if necessary.

5 Create cracks in the block. (See photo for placement and Special Techniques, page 8.)

6 Dilute some modeling paste with water (about one part water to three parts paste) and use a fan brush to brush the mixture into the cracks, sealing them but not filling them up.

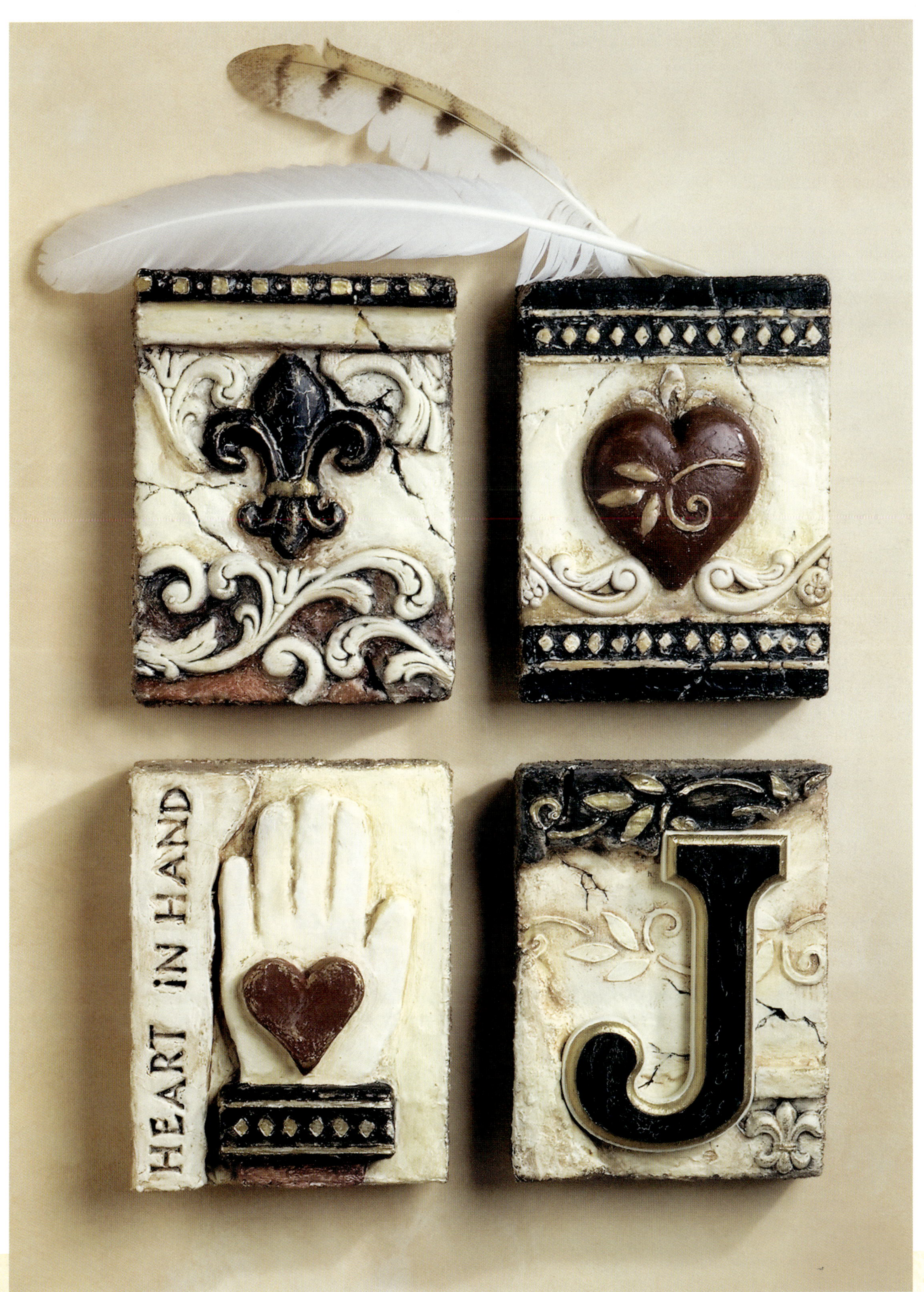
HEART IN HAND

7 Basecoat the back of the block Lamp Black. Basecoat the remaining area of the block Lt. Buttermilk, including all embellishments (see figure a).

8 Apply weathered wood crackling medium to the fleur-de-lis, following manufacturer's instructions. Paint the fleur-de-lis and top edge of the block Lamp Black. Paint the stenciled areas Glorious Gold. For a more weathered look, after drying, lightly sand the stenciled areas, removing some paint.

9 Brush on Rookwood Red under the 1¼" ledge and wipe off with a soft cloth.

10 Brush Rookwood Red into areas around wood pieces at the bottom of the block. Wipe off, leaving some color (see figure b). Brush Shadow Tan over the remaining Lt. Buttermilk areas on the front of the block and wipe, leaving some color, particularly in crevices (see figure c). Repeat with Golden Halo and Earth Brown (see figure d). Brush Soft Black around all wood pieces and into cracks and wipe off, leaving color in crevices (see figure e).

11 Lightly brush Buttermilk across the tops of the wood pieces to highlight (see figure f).

Modeling paste layer

12 Paint the center band on the fleur-de-lis and add highlights on raised areas with Glorious Gold (see photo.)

13 Brush on and wipe off Soft Black on the sides of the block.

14 Dip a sponge in Earth Brown, blot and sponge randomly on the sides of the block. Repeat at random with Shadow Tan, Soft Black, Lt. Buttermilk and Glorious Gold, changing colors on the sponge. Continue until you are satisfied with the effect (see photo).

Finishing

1 Allow to dry thoroughly.

2 Seal with multi-purpose sealer.

Basecoat Lt. Buttermilk.

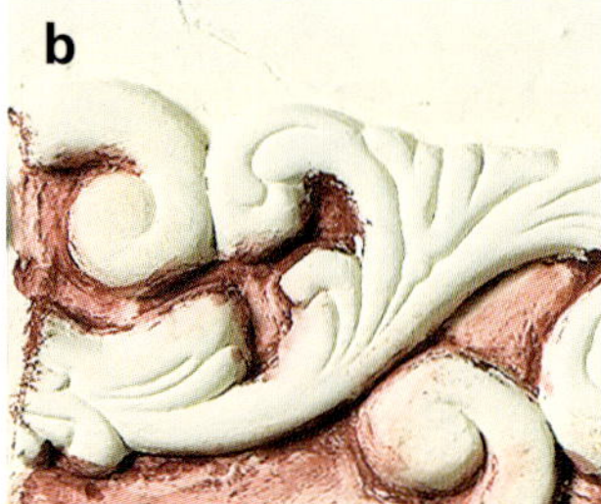

Antique Rookwood Red around wood pieces at bottom.

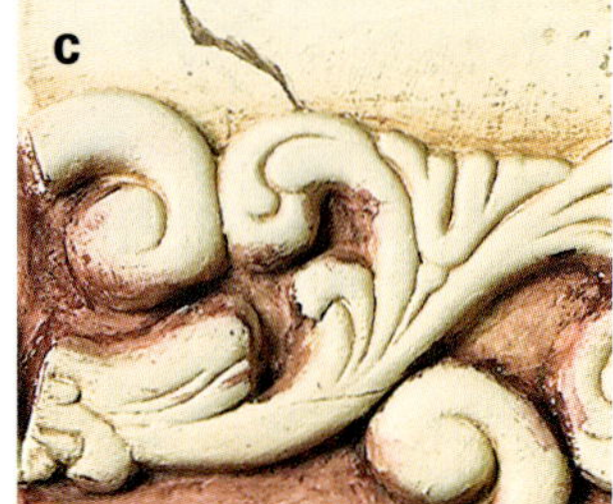

Antique remaining Lt. Buttermilk areas with Shadow Tan.

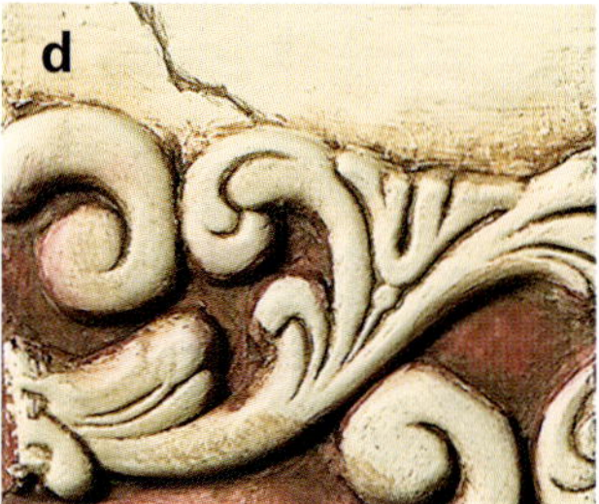

Antique same areas with Golden Halo and Earth Brown.

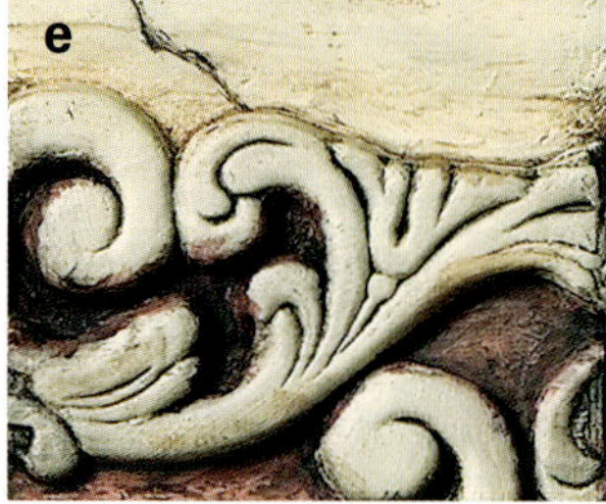

Antique Soft Black around wood pieces.

Lightly brush Buttermilk over wood pieces.

Cut the decorative wood piece as indicated below; modeling paste layer (photo left) shows placement on project.

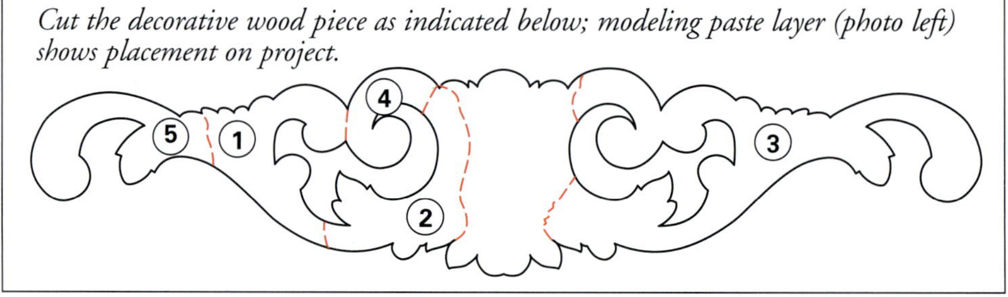

Modeling paste layer

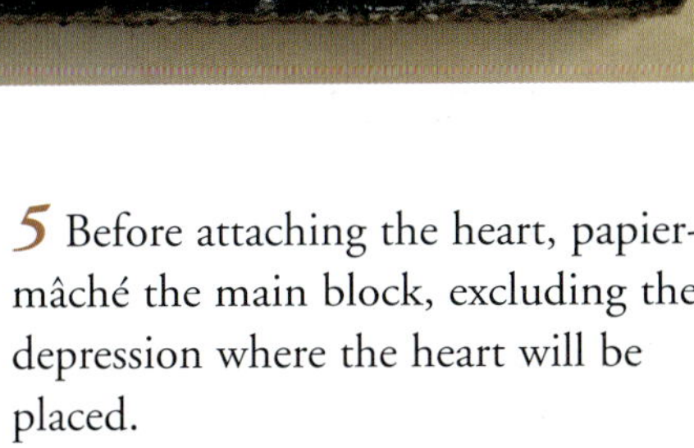

HEART

MATERIALS

SURFACE

1" styrofoam, 6" x 8"
½" styrofoam, 6" x 8"

PAINTS

DecoArt Americana Acrylic Paints
Lamp Black
Lt. Buttermilk
Rookwood Red
DecoArt Heavenly Hues
Earth Brown
Golden Halo
Shadow Tan
Soft Black
DecoArt Dazzling Metallics
Glorious Gold

BRUSHES

Loew-Cornell, Inc.
½" and 1" wash/glaze: *Series 7550*
#6 round: *Series 7000*
#00 fan: *Series 7200*

SUPPLIES

Foam puffy heart (3½"x 3¼") by *Kreative Foam*
Liquitex Modeling Paste
Liquitex Matte Gel Medium
Decorative wood piece by *Walnut Hollow Classic Dimensions #16406*
Craft saw
Stencil by *Plaid Simply Stencil #28178 Classic Fleur-de-lis Collection*
Stencil by *Plaid Simply Stencil #28172 Scrolling Vine*
Stencil by *Plaid Simply Stencil #28171 Fleur-de-lis*
Soft cloth or paper towels
Cotton swabs
Stencil sponges or makeup sponges
Sandpaper (fine)
DecoArt Multi-Purpose Sealer

INSTRUCTIONS

Preparation

1 Read Basic Techniques, pages 4-7.

2 Glue the ½" and 1" styrofoam 6" x 8" blocks together using modeling paste. Create a hanging hole for the back 1½" down from the center top.

3 For the scrollwork under the heart, measure and mark off with a pencil 2 7/16" from each end of the decorative wood piece. Cut along the line with a craft saw. Sand the raw edges.

4 Remove the hanger from the foam heart for the center of the block. Cut the heart shape in half with a *Wonder Cutter*, or if you prefer, create a depression in the block deep enough to accommodate half of the shape. (See Special Techniques, page 10.)

5 Before attaching the heart, papier-mâché the main block, excluding the depression where the heart will be placed.

Modeling and Painting

1 Coat the block with a layer of modeling paste (excluding the depression).

2 When dry, use modeling paste and *Fleur-de-lis Stencil #28171* to apply the small fleur-de-lis above the area where the heart will be placed. (See Special Techniques, page 10.) Optional: When the fleur-de-lis is dry, carve an oval groove in the center (see photo).

3 Measure ½" from the top and bottom of the block and stencil the top and bottom borders using the border of the *Classic Fleur-de-lis Stencil #28178*. When dry, lightly sand the stenciled areas, if necessary.

4 Texture the sides of the block.

5 Use modeling paste to secure the heart in the depression (or adhere the half heart). Smooth edges with a wet brush. Apply the *Scrolling Vine Stencil*

Antique Earth Brown over Lt. Buttermilk basecoat.

Antique same areas with Golden Halo, Shadow Tan and Soft Black. Paint raised border areas Glorious Gold.

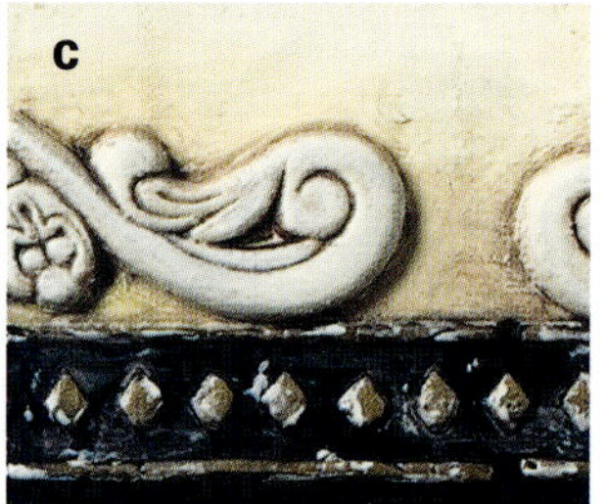

Lightly brush stencil areas and wood pieces with Lt. Buttermilk.

Randomly sponge and blot with Earth Brown and Shadow Tan.

Repeat at random with Soft Black and Lt. Buttermilk.

Repeat at random with Glorious Gold.

#28172 design on the heart using modeling paste.

6 Spread a 1/8" layer of modeling paste in the areas where the decorative wood pieces will be placed (refer to photo).

7 Press the two wood pieces into the modeling paste as shown in photo. Fill gaps under edges if necessary. (See Special Techniques, page 9.)

8 Create cracks in the block. (See photo for placement and refer to Special Techniques, page 8.)

9 Dilute some modeling paste with water (about one part water to three parts paste) and use a fan brush to brush into the cracks, sealing them but not filling them up.

10 Basecoat the back of the block and top and bottom stenciled areas with Lamp Black. Basecoat the remaining areas Lt. Buttermilk, including all embellishments.

11 Brush the Lt. Buttermilk areas on the front of the block with Earth Brown; wipe off with a soft cloth, leaving color in the crevices (see figure a). Repeat with Golden Halo, Shadow Tan and Soft Black until achieving a weathered effect (see figure b).

12 Avoiding stenciled area, paint the heart Rookwood Red. Paint stenciled design on the heart Glorious Gold.

13 Paint raised areas of the border Glorious Gold. When dry, brush across lightly with Lt. Buttermilk.

14 Brush across the tops of the wood pieces lightly with Lt. Buttermilk to highlight (see figure c).

15 Dip the sponge in Earth Brown; blot and sponge randomly on the sides of the block (see figure d). Repeat at random with Shadow Tan, Soft Black, and Lt. Buttermilk, changing colors on the sponge (see figure e). Lastly, sponge with Glorious Gold, until satisfied with the effect (see figure f).

Finishing

1 Allow to dry thoroughly.

2 Seal with multi-purpose sealer.

HEART IN HAND

MATERIALS

SURFACE

1" styrofoam, 6" x 8"
1/2" styrofoam, 6" x 20"

PAINTS

DecoArt Americana Acrylic Paints
Lamp Black
Lt. Buttermilk
Rookwood Red
DecoArt Heavenly Hues
Earth Brown
Golden Halo
Shadow Tan
Soft Black
DecoArt Dazzling Metallics
Glorious Gold

BRUSHES

Loew-Cornell, Inc.
1/2" and 1" wash/glaze: *Series 7550*
#6 round: *Series 7000*

SUPPLIES

Tracing and transfer paper
Liquitex Modeling Paste
Liquitex Matte Gel Medium
Stone stamps by *Milestones*
Traditional Style Letter & Number Stone Stamps
Stencil by *Plaid Simply Stencil #28178 Classic Fleur-de-lis*
Soft cloth or paper towels
Cotton swabs
Stencil sponges or makeup sponges
Sandpaper (medium)
DecoArt Multi-Purpose Sealer

INSTRUCTIONS

Preparation

1 Read Basic Techniques, pages 4-7.

2 Cut a 6" x 8" block from the 1/2" styrofoam. Glue the 1/2" styrofoam block to the 1" block using modeling paste.

3 Create a hanging hole for the back approximately 1½" down from the center top.

4 Trace the project patterns on page 27 onto tracing paper and use transfer paper to transfer onto the ½" styrofoam. Cut out the shapes using a serrated knife.

5 Shape the edges of the heart using your fingers to compress them. Shape the hand by compressing the edges, rounding the fingers of the hand and deepening and rounding the depressions between the fingers. Shape the edges of the broken piece by compressing with fingers as needed to fit next to the side of the hand.

6 Using modeling paste, attach the heart shape to the middle of the hand. Attach the 3¼" x 1⅜" rectangle (representing the sleeve cuff) ½" above the bottom of the hand, aligning it with the hand cutout. Attach the broken piece to the left front of the block (see photo), then attach the hand unit next to the broken edge.

7 Papier-mâché the entire surface, pressing the papier-mâché carefully into the crevices and around shapes.

Modeling and Painting

1 Trace the pattern for the "HEART IN HAND" lettering on tracing paper and transfer to the front of the broken piece, using transfer paper. Use stone stamps to create lettering (see figs. a-c and also Special Techniques, page 11). Following this step, coat any remaining areas of the block with a layer of modeling paste. Smooth the surface using a soft brush dipped in water.

2 When dry, use modeling paste and *Classic Fleur-de-lis Stencil #28178* to stencil the pattern on the cuff. Lightly sand stenciled areas, if necessary. (See Special Techniques, page 10).

3 Texture the sides of the block.

4 Basecoat the back of the block and all sides of the cuff with Lamp Black. Basecoat the remaining areas and heart Lt. Buttermilk (see figure d).

5 Paint the heart Rookwood Red (see figure e). Brush Rookwood Red on the bottom of the hand unit under the cuff and wipe with a soft cloth, leaving some color.

6 Brush both the Lt. Buttermilk areas

Modeling paste layer

Press letters into dry papier-mâché layer.

Fill with modeling paste.

Press stone stamp letters into set modeling paste.

Basecoat Lt. Buttermilk.

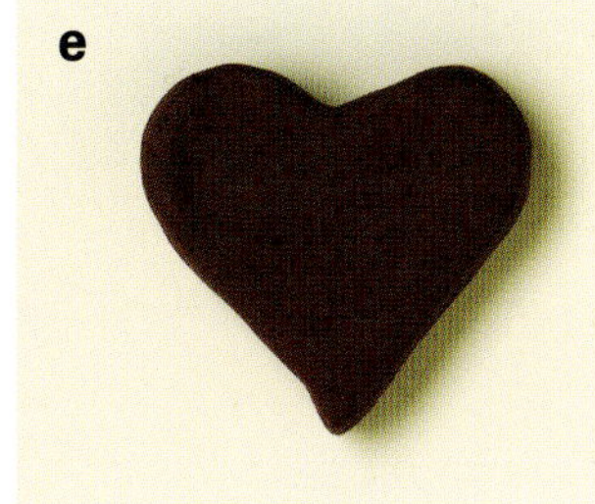

Paint Rookwood Red.

Highlight sides and top with Glorious Gold.

on the front of the block and the Rookwood Red area under the cuff with Earth Brown; wipe off, leaving color in the crevices. Repeat with Golden Halo, Shadow Tan and Soft Black until achieving a weathered effect (see photo).

7 Brush the sides of the block with Soft Black and wipe off.

8 Paint the stenciled design on the cuff Glorious Gold. Sand lightly when dry to create a more weathered look. Lightly brush the sides and top of heart with Glorious Gold to highlight (see figure f).

9 Dip the sponge in Earth Brown, blot and sponge randomly on the sides of the block. Repeat at random with Shadow Tan, Soft Black, Lt. Buttermilk and Glorious Gold, changing colors on the sponge. Continue until satisfied with the effect (see photo).

Finishing

1 Allow to dry thoroughly.

2 Seal with multi-purpose sealer.

MATERIALS

SURFACE

1" styrofoam, 6" x 8"
½" styrofoam, 6" x 12"

PAINTS

DecoArt Americana Acrylic Paints
Lamp Black
Lt. Buttermilk
DecoArt Heavenly Hues
Earth Brown
Golden Halo
Shadow Tan
Soft Black
DecoArt Dazzling Metallics
Glorious Gold

BRUSHES

Loew-Cornell, Inc.
½" and 1" wash/glaze: *Series 7550*
#6 round: *Series 7000*
#00 fan: *Series 7200*

SUPPLIES

Tracing and transfer paper
Liquitex Modeling Paste
Liquitex Matte Gel Medium
6" wood letter by *Juma Farms, Ltd.*
Decorative wood piece by *Walnut Hollow Classic Dimensions #16110 Fleur-de-lis*
Stencil by *Plaid Simply Stencil #28172 Scrolling Vine*
Soft cloth or paper towels
Cotton swabs
Stencil sponges or makeup sponges
Sandpaper (medium)
Tacky glue
DecoArt Weathered Wood Crackling Medium
DecoArt Multi-Purpose Sealer

INSTRUCTIONS

Note: You can easily adapt the basic design of this block to accommodate any letter of the alphabet. Find patterns for all 26 letters of the alphabet on pages 38-39 or create your own designs substituting with stencils of your choice.

Preparation

1 Read Basic Techniques, pages 4-7.

Modeling paste layer

2 Cut a 6"x 8" block from the ½" styrofoam and also a 6" x ½" strip (the length of this strip will be re-cut to fit with your specific letter). Set the ½" styrofoam aside to use for creating broken pieces around your letter. These pieces will be custom cut for your specific letter.

3 Glue the 1" and ½" thick blocks together using modeling paste. Create a hanging hole for the back approximately 1½" down from the center top.

4 If you prefer, you may trace and transfer the pattern on page 38 (enlarging it 350%), otherwise proceed as follows. Draw a 6" x 8" rectangle on tracing paper to represent the block. Lay the wood letter inside the rectangle, centering it within the area and trace around it. Draw two "broken" shapes and a bar (if desired) to fit around the letter. Transfer the two "broken" shapes onto ½" styrofoam and cut out using a serrated knife. Cut the bar to fit. Shape the edges of the "broken" pieces using your fingers to compress them.

5 Place all shapes including the letter and fleur-de-lis onto the block and fit carefully. Remove the letter and fleur-de-lis and glue the remaining shapes and the bar to the block using modeling paste.

6 Papier-mâché the entire surface, pressing the papier-mâché carefully around the shapes.

Modeling and Painting

1 Cover the entire block with a layer of modeling paste. Texture the sides including the sides of broken pieces.

2 When dry, use modeling paste and *Scrolling Vine Stencil #28172* to apply the vine pattern on the front of the block and on one of the broken pieces. (See Special Techniques, page 10.) Lightly sand the stenciled areas, if necessary.

Basecoat letter Lt. Buttermilk.

Paint middle edge Glorious Gold.

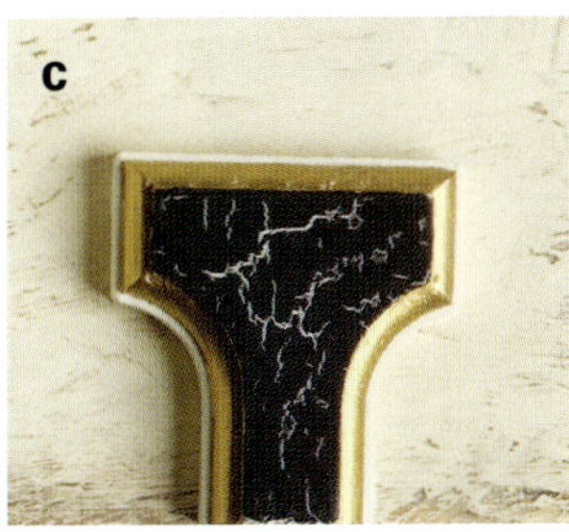

Apply weathered wood medium to top surface, then Lamp Black.

Basecoat Lamp Black and Lt. Buttermilk.

Apply Glorious Gold on raised stencil areas. Antique Earth Brown over Lt. Buttermilk.

Antique with Golden Halo, Shadow Tan, and Soft Black.

3 Attach the fleur-de-lis decorative wood piece using modeling paste. (See Special Techniques, page 9.)

4 Create cracks in the block. (See Special Techniques, page 8.) Dilute some modeling paste with water (about one part water to three parts paste) and use a fan brush to brush into the cracks, sealing them but not filling them up.

5 Paint the wood letter Lt. Buttermilk (see figure a). Paint the middle curved edge with Glorious Gold, leaving Lt. Buttermilk on the bottom edge (see figure b). When dry, coat the front surface of the letter with weathered wood crackling medium, following manufacturer's instructions. Top coat the front with Lamp Black (see figure c).

6 Basecoat the back of the block and the top broken shape with Lamp Black. Basecoat the remaining areas Lt. Buttermilk (see figure d).

7 Paint the raised stenciled areas on the broken piece Glorious Gold (see figure e). To create a more weathered look, sand lightly to remove some paint.

8 Brush the Lt. Buttermilk areas on the front of the block with Earth Brown; wipe with a soft cloth, leaving color in the crevices (see figure e). Repeat with Golden Halo, Shadow Tan and Soft Black until a weathered effect is achieved (see figure f).

9 Brush Soft Black on the sides of the block and wipe.

10 Dip the sponge in Earth Brown, blot and sponge randomly on the sides of the block. Repeat at random with Shadow Tan, Soft Black, Lt. Buttermilk and Glorious Gold, changing colors on the sponge. Continue until the desired effect is achieved (see photo).

Finishing

1 Allow to dry thoroughly. Glue the letter in place using tacky glue.

2 Seal with multi-purpose sealer.

THE ALPHABET IN STONE

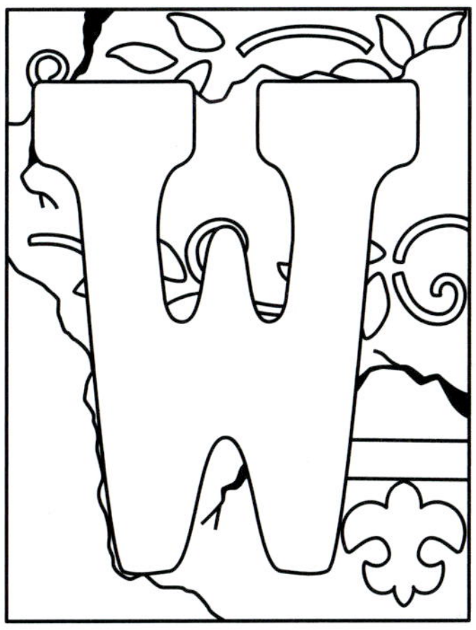

Personalize your stone creation by adapting the basic design of the "Letter J" block on page 36 to accommodate any letter of the alphabet. Use the patterns presented here for all 26 letters of the alphabet (enlarge 350 percent for actual size) or create your own designs using the stencils and embellishments of your choice.

NATURE'S SPLENDOR

It is the marriage of the soul with Nature that makes the intellect fruitful, and gives birth to imagination. —Thoreau

LEAF

MATERIALS

SURFACE

2" styrofoam block, 4" x 4"

PAINTS

DecoArt Americana Acrylic Paints
Payne's Grey
Violet Haze
Wisteria
DecoArt Dazzling Metallics
Bronze
Glorious Gold
Shimmering Silver
DecoArt Heavenly Hues
Soft Black

BRUSHES

Loew-Cornell, Inc.
½" and 1" wash/glaze: *Series 7550*
#00 fan: *Series 7200*

SUPPLIES

Plaid Faster Plaster, 7.68 oz. package
Plaid Faster Plaster Mold #67479 and #67484
Liquitex Modeling Paste
Liquitex Matte Gel Medium
Spoon or dull gouging instrument
Stencil sponges or makeup sponges
Cotton swabs
Soft cloth or paper towels
DecoArt Multi-Purpose Sealer
Tacky glue

INSTRUCTIONS

Preparation

1 Read Basic Techniques, pages 4-7.

2 Measure 1" in from all sides and create a square shape in the center of the 4" x 4" block by scoring with a pencil tip. Use a serrated knife to cut about ⅜" into the styrofoam and remove styrofoam from inside the square using a dull instrument such as the end of a spoon. Finish the edges of the block by shaping with your fingers.

3 Create plaster pieces using molds and following manufacturer's instructions. (See Special Techniques, page 9.) Use the square form from mold #67484 and the leaf from #67479.

4 Break the square plaster piece by scoring the back and snapping (see photo for pieces used on project).

5 Place a hole for hanging on the back, approximately ½" from the top.

6 Papier-mâché the entire block and allow to dry.

Modeling and Painting

1 Coat the block with a layer of modeling paste. Smooth the surface using a soft brush dipped in water. Let dry.

2 Attach the broken plaster pieces to the block using modeling paste. Refer to the photo for placement.

3 Use a serrated knife to create cracks, referring to photos for placement. (See Special Techniques, page 8.) Dilute modeling paste with water (about one part water to three parts paste) and use a fan brush to brush paste into the cracks to seal but not to fill them.

4 Basecoat the leaf with Shimmering

Modeling paste layer

Silver (see figure a). When dry, brush on Soft Black and wipe off with a soft cloth (see figure b). Use a cotton swab to carefully wipe the surface, leaving color in the crevices. Use a cotton swab to add a small amount of both Bronze and Glorious Gold to the surface of the leaf (see figure c).

5 Basecoat the block and plaster pieces with Payne's Grey (see figure d).

6 Randomly sponge the following colors on the front of the block: Bronze, Shimmering Silver, Violet Haze and Wisteria (see figure e). The predominant colors on the front of the block will be Violet Haze and Wisteria. Leave the center square mostly dark with some Bronze brushed on. Brush Bronze into some of the cracks (see figure f).

7 Sponge the same colors (Bronze, Shimmering Silver, Violet Haze and Wisteria) sparingly on the sides of the block. Brush Bronze into some cracks.

Finishing

1 Attach the leaf using tacky glue.

2 Seal with multi-purpose sealer.

ACORN

MATERIALS

SURFACE

2" styrofoam block, 4" x 4"

PAINTS

DecoArt Americana Acrylic Paints
Black Green
Green Mist
DecoArt Dazzling Metallics
Bronze
Glorious Gold
Venetian Gold
DecoArt Heavenly Hues
Soft Black
Patina Green

BRUSHES

Loew-Cornell, Inc.
½" and 1" wash/glaze: *Series 7550*
#00 fan: *Series 7200*

SUPPLIES

Liquitex Modeling Paste
Liquitex Matte Gel Medium
Plaid Faster Plaster, 7.68 oz. package
Plaid Faster Plaster Mold #67479 and #67484
Spoon or dull gouging instrument
Stencil sponges or makeup sponges
Cotton swabs
Soft cloth or paper towels
DecoArt Multi-Purpose Sealer
Tacky glue

a
Basecoat Shimmering Silver.

b
Antique with Soft Black, leaving color in crevices.

c
Add Bronze and Glorious Gold accents.

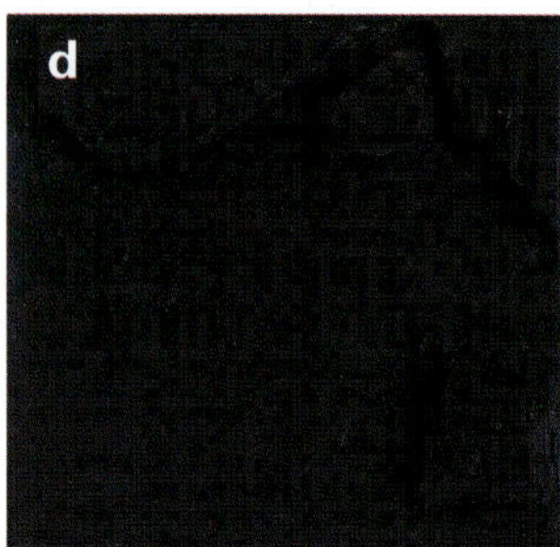
d
Basecoat Payne's Grey.

e
Randomly sponge Bronze, Shimmering Silver, Violet Haze and Wisteria.

f
Sponge and wipe Bronze around plaster pieces and brush into cracks.

INSTRUCTIONS

Preparation

1 Read Basic Techniques, pages 4-7.

2 Measure 1" in from all sides and create a square shape in the center of the square block by scoring with a pencil tip. Use a serrated knife to cut about ⅜" into the styrofoam and remove the styrofoam from the square using a dull instrument such as a spoon. Finish the square by shaping with fingers.

3 Create plaster pieces using molds and following manufacturer's instructions. (See Special Techniques, page 9.) Use the square form and the corner form from mold #67484 and the acorn from #67479.

4 Break the corner and square plaster pieces by scoring the back and snapping (see photo for pieces used on project.)

5 Place a hole for hanging on the back, approximately ½" from top.

6 Papier-mâché the entire block and allow to dry.

Modeling and Painting

1 Coat the block with a layer of modeling paste. Smooth the surface using a soft brush dipped in water. Let dry.

2 Attach the broken plaster pieces to the block using modeling paste. Refer to photo for placement.

3 Create cracks using a serrated knife (see photos for placement and Special Techniques, page 8.) Dilute modeling paste with water (about one part water to three parts paste) and use a fan

brush to brush paste into the cracks to seal. Be careful not to fill the cracks.

4 Paint the cap of the acorn with Bronze (see figure a). Paint the bottom of the acorn with Glorious Gold (see figure b). When dry, brush on and gently wipe off Soft Black with a cotton swab, leaving color in the crevices (see figure c).

5 Basecoat the block and plaster pieces with Black Green (see figure d).

6 Randomly sponge the following colors on the front of the block: Venetian Gold, Glorious Gold, Green Mist, and Patina Green (see figure e). The predominant color will be green. Sponge and wipe Venetian Gold around the plaster pieces, allowing the gold to remain in some crevices (see figure f). Sponge again with greens, if necessary. Sponge the colors sparingly inside the center square, allowing it to remain darker. Using the fan brush, add Venetian Gold inside some of the cracks.

7 Sponge the same colors (Venetian Gold, Glorious Gold, Green Mist, and Patina Green) sparingly on the sides. Brush Venetian Gold into some cracks (see photo).

Finishing

1 Glue the acorn in place using tacky glue.

2 Seal with multi-purpose sealer.

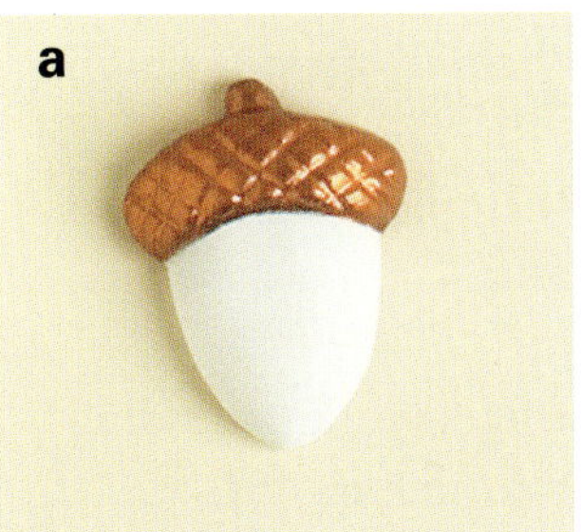

Paint the cap Bronze.

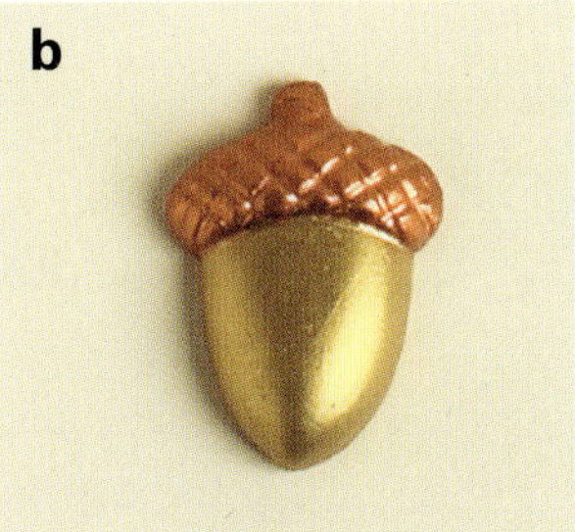

Paint the bottom Glorious Gold.

Antique with Soft Black, leaving color in the crevices.

Modeling paste layer

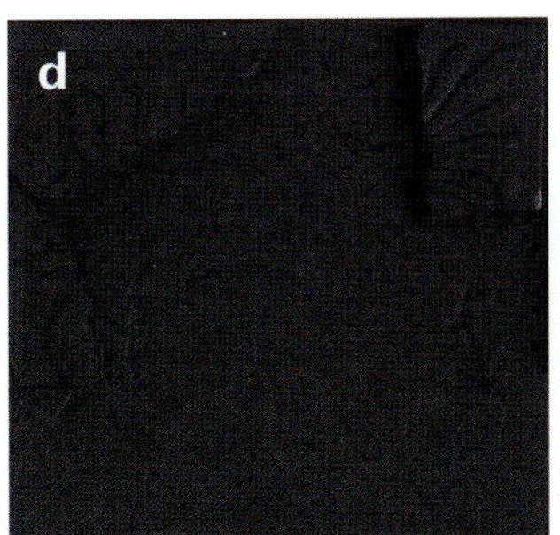

Basecoat Black Green.

Randomly sponge Venetian Gold, Glorious Gold, Green Mist, and Patina Green.

Sponge and wipe Venetian Gold around plaster pieces and brush into cracks.

NATURAL REFLECTIONS

You use a glass mirror to see your face: you use works of art to see your soul. —George Bernard Shaw

MATERIALS

SURFACE

1" styrofoam disk, 8" diameter

PAINTS

DecoArt Americana Acrylic Paints
Desert Turquoise
Rookwood Red
DecoArt Heavenly Hues
Purple Heather
Soft Black
DecoArt Dazzling Metallics
Bronze
Glorious Gold

BRUSHES

Loew-Cornell, Inc.
½" and 1" wash/glaze: *Series 7550*
#6 round: *Series 7000*

SUPPLIES

Tracing and transfer paper
Styrofoam scraps
Liquitex Modeling Paste
Liquitex Matte Gel Medium
4" round mirror
Sandpaper (medium)
2" x 1½" dragonfly by *Kreative Foam*
Grape stencil by *Plaid Simply Stencil #28113 Bunches of Grapes*
Gold foil by *Delta Renaissance Foil Easy Gold Leafing System*
Silver foil by *Delta Renaissance Foil Easy Gold Leafing System*
Delta Renaissance Foil Adhesive
Delta Renaissance Foil Dimensional Adhesive
Tacky glue
Stencil sponges or makeup sponges
Soft cloth or paper towels
DecoArt Multi-Purpose Sealer

INSTRUCTIONS

Preparation

1 Read Basic Techniques, pages 4-7.

2 Center the 4" mirror on the styrofoam disk and score a line around the edge, using a pencil tip. Remove mirror. Dig out a ⅛" depression in the styrofoam inside the circle. Use another piece of styrofoam to smooth the area.

3 Place a hole for hanging in the back of the disk about ¾" from the edge.

4 Papier-mâché the disk (excluding the depression for the mirror).

Modeling and Painting

1 Coat the entire disk with a layer of modeling paste, including the depression for the mirror. Press the mirror in place, keeping it flush with the surface. The modeling paste will adhere the mirror to the disk. Texture the edge of the disk. Let dry.

2 Basecoat the dragonfly with Desert Turquoise. Apply foil adhesive to the top of the dragonfly and foil with Silver, following manufacturer's instructions (see figure a). Brush Glorious Gold over the tops of the tail. Randomly brush small amounts of

Modeling paste layer

a — Apply Silver foil.

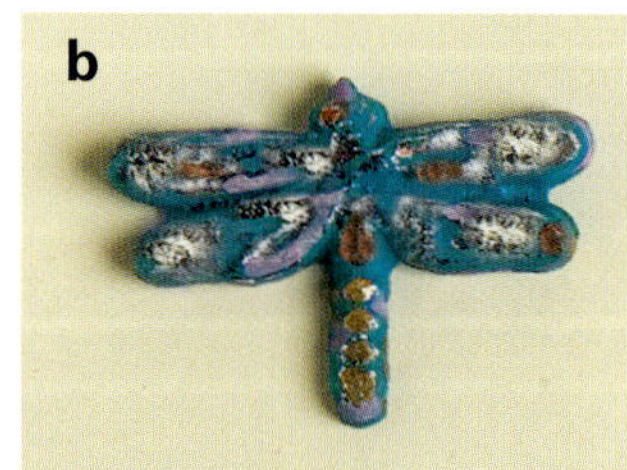

b — Dab Glorious Gold on tail, then Purple Heather and Bronze randomly overall.

c — Antique Soft Black.

Purple Heather and Bronze on the dragonfly (see figure b). Brush on and wipe off Soft Black (see figure c). Seal when dry.

3 Trace the pattern on page 29 onto tracing paper and transfer to the disk using transfer paper. Keep in mind the position of your hanging hole at the top of the piece.

4 Using modeling paste and stencil #28113, stencil the grape and leaf shapes. (See Special Techniques, page 10.) Sand raised areas lightly when dry, if necessary.

5 Basecoat the disk Glorious Gold. Let dry.

6 Brush on Rookwood Red over the front and sides of the disk and wipe off with a soft cloth (see figure d).

7 Dip a sponge into Glorious Gold, blot and sponge onto the sides of disk.

8 Run a bead of dimensional adhesive around the edge of the mirror and foil with Gold, following manufacturer's instructions.

9 Apply foil adhesive to the surfaces of the stenciled areas and foil with Gold (see figure e).

10 Apply dots of dimensional adhesive about 1/8" apart on top of the Gold foil area around the mirror. Foil dots with Silver leaf. When dry, seal all foiled areas.

11 Brush on and wipe off Soft Black over the front and sides of the mirror (see figure f).

Finishing

1 Glue the dragonfly in place, using tacky glue (see pattern).

2 Seal with multi-purpose sealer.

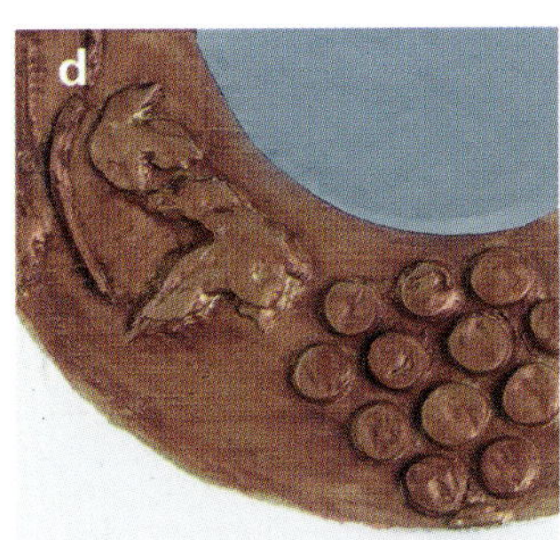

Antique Rookwood Red.

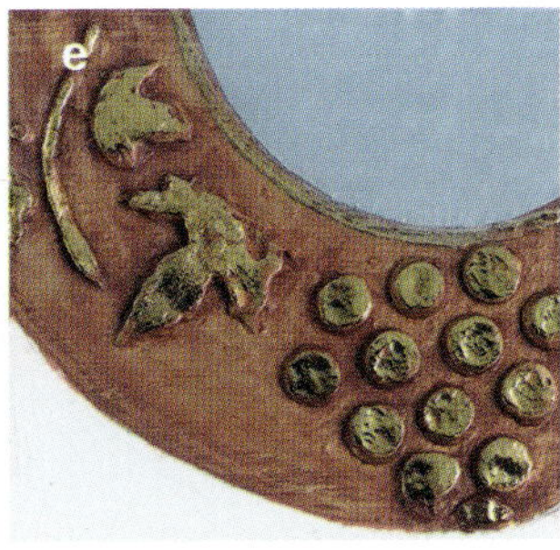

Apply Gold foil.

Antique Soft Black.

PRECIOUS FRAGMENTS

To every thing there is a season, and a time to every purpose under the heaven. —Ecclesiastes 3:1

ROMAN

MATERIALS

SURFACE

1" styrofoam, 12" x 18"
½" styrofoam, 4" x 18"

PAINTS

DecoArt Americana Acrylic Paints
Lt. Buttermilk
DecoArt Heavenly Hues
Earth Brown
Golden Halo
Shadow Tan
Soft Black

BRUSHES

Loew-Cornell, Inc.
½" and 1" wash/glaze: *Series 7550*
#6 round: *Series 7000*
#00 fan: *Series 7200*

SUPPLIES

Tracing and transfer paper
Liquitex Modeling Paste
Liquitex Matte Gel Medium
Plaid Faster Plaster Molds #67484, #67479, #67259
Plaid Faster Plaster, two 7.68 oz. bags for each project or equivalent
Soft cloth or paper towels
Cotton swabs
DecoArt Multi-Purpose Sealer

INSTRUCTIONS

Preparation

1 Read Basic Techniques, pages 4-7.

2 Cut a 5" x 15" block from 1" styrofoam. Break off the bottom right corner of the block as shown in the photo. (See Special Techniques, page 8). Cut notches in the left side using the pattern on page 48 as your guide.

3 Create two holes for hanging in the back of the block; space them about 6" apart and ¾" from the top.

4 Cut a 1¼" x 15" strip from ½" styrofoam, then cut a second strip ½" x 14".

5 On the front of the block, use modeling paste to attach the 1¼" x 15" strip, aligning it with the top edge. Trim the right edge of the strip to match the broken edge of the block. Position the second strip below the first, aligning the left edge with the notched left edge of the block. Break off the right edge so that it is about ¾" shorter than the broken right edge of the block. Set aside.

6 Follow manufacturer's instructions for mixing plaster, then pour the following into the required molds: two corners, an oval, two scallops and a frame. (See Special Techniques, page 9.) Break up the frame at the corners to make the top border. Fit the last piece of the frame section to the broken edge and break to fit. Break one piece of a corner section for the right side. It does not have to fit evenly at the broken edge (see photo). Set plaster pieces aside.

7 Papier-mâché the block, covering the attached strips and the inside areas of the holes on the back.

Modeling and Painting

1 Coat the entire piece with a layer of modeling paste.

2 Attach all plaster pieces to the block using modeling paste and referring to the photo for placement.

3 Create cracks using a serrated knife. (See Special Techniques, page 8.)

4 Basecoat the piece using Lt. Buttermilk. When dry, brush on Soft Black in the cracks and wipe off with a soft cloth. Repeat with Earth Brown (see figure a).

5 Brush on and wipe off Golden Halo over the front and sides of the piece, allowing color to remain in the crevices (see figure b). Repeat with Shadow Tan. (see figure c). Brush on and wipe off Soft Black on the sides.

Finishing

1 When thoroughly dry, seal with multi-purpose sealer.

Modeling paste layer

Antique Soft Black into cracks. Antique Earth Brown over front.

Antique Golden Halo over front.

Antique Shadow Tan over front.

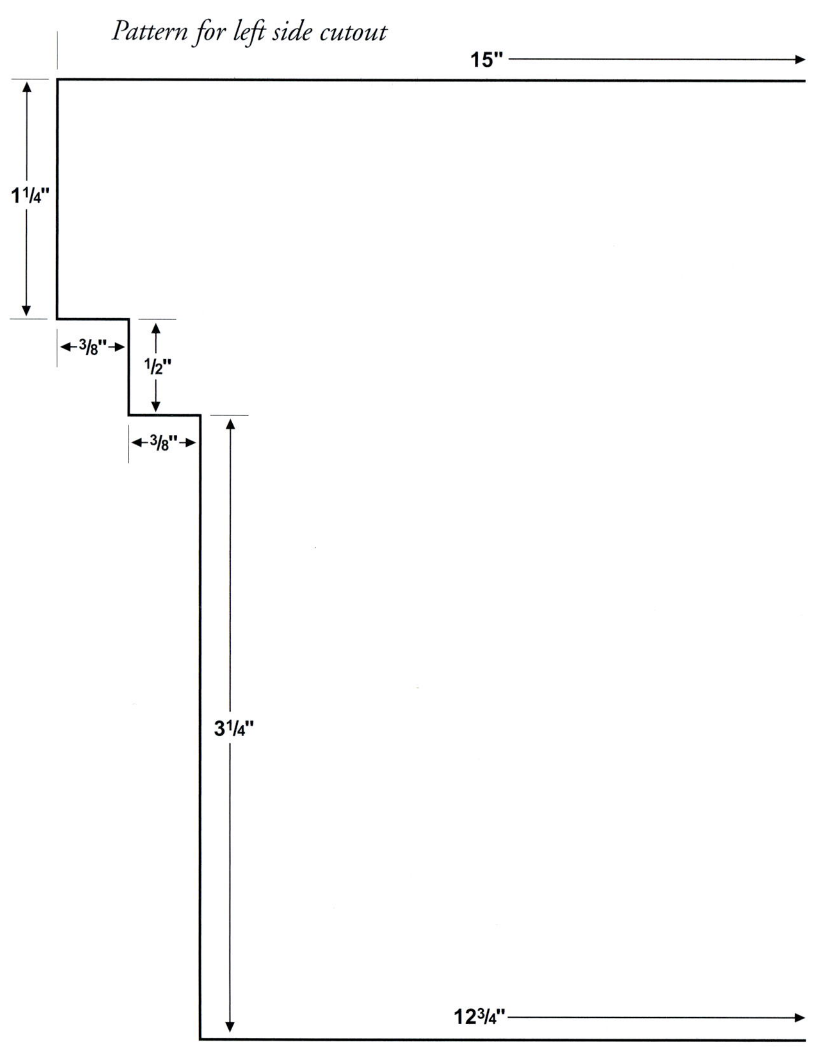

AZTEC

The variation shown in the photo on this page makes use of the Roman Fragment wall hanging but gives it a utilitarian purpose by attaching it to a planter box. For more variety, a terra cotta finish replaces the antique ivory finish of the original piece.

MATERIALS

(See list for Roman)
Additional:
1" styrofoam, 12" x 24"
Wood skewers

PAINTS

(For terra cotta finish)
DecoArt Americana Acrylic Paints
Soft Peach
DecoArt Dazzling Metallics
Glorious Gold
DecoArt Heavenly Hues
Angel Flesh
Earth Brown
Shadow Tan
Soft Black
Terra Cotta

Box Construction

1 Read Basic Techniques, pages 4-7.

2 Use 1" styrofoam to cut pieces as follows:
- a) Bottom piece: 12" x 4½"
- b) Back piece: 12" x 3¾"
- c) Two side pieces: 3½" x 3¾"

3 Smooth edges using another piece of styrofoam like a sanding block.

4 Use modeling paste to glue pieces together. Place the bottom piece on a level surface and attach the back piece to the top surface, lining up the outside edges. Add the sides, perpendicular to the back, again placing them on the top surface of the bottom piece. Fit in place and adhere to both the bottom and the back. (The front of the box will be the Roman Fragment.) Inserting wood skewers about 4" in length or the stick part of cotton swabs will help secure the pieces. Allow to dry.

5 Papier-mâché all sides.

Modeling and Painting

1 Coat the box with a layer of modeling paste, avoiding the open ends that will be attached to the front wall fragment (see photo).

2 Construct the front Roman Fragment following instructions beginning on page 46; however, exclude the holes for hanging.

3 When dry, use modeling paste to attach the box to the back of the wall fragment, centering the back box. Remove excess modeling paste at the joint using a cotton swab or wet brush.

4 Basecoat all areas Soft Peach including the inside and bottom (see figure a). When dry, on the fragment front only, brush on Soft Black in the cracks and wipe off with a soft cloth. Repeat with Earth Brown.

5 Brush on Terra Cotta and Earth Brown on entire piece and wipe off with a soft cloth until desired effect is achieved (see figure b). Brush on and wipe off Shadow Tan and Angel Flesh (see figure c).

6 Dip a sponge into Glorious Gold, blot and sweep color across the top border and in random areas on the front of the plaster pieces (see figure c).

Finishing

1 When thoroughly dry, seal with multi-purpose sealer.

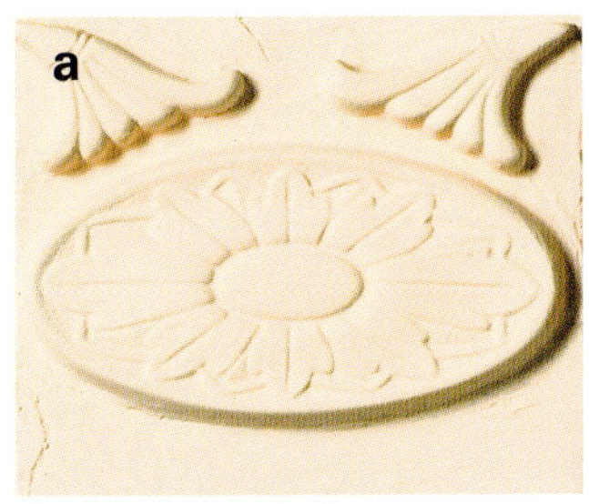

Basecoat Soft Peach.

Antique Terra Cotta and Earth Brown.

Antique Shadow Tan and Angel Flesh. Randomly sponge Glorious Gold on plaster pieces.

DOGWOOD

MATERIALS

SURFACE

1" styrofoam, 6" x 8"
½" styrofoam, 6" x 8"

PAINTS

DecoArt Americana Acrylic Paints
Lamp Black
Lt. Buttermilk
DecoArt Heavenly Hues
Earth Brown
Golden Halo
Shadow Tan
Soft Black
DecoArt Dazzling Metallics
Glorious Gold

BRUSHES

Loew-Cornell, Inc.
½" and 1" wash/glaze: *Series 7550*
#6 round: *Series 7000*
#00 fan: *Series 7200*

SUPPLIES

Liquitex Modeling Paste
Liquitex Matte Gel Medium
Flowers and leaves by *Kreative Foam*
DecoArt Perfect Crackle (two-step)
Cotton swabs
Stencil sponges or makeup sponges
Soft cloth or paper towels
DecoArt Multi-Purpose Sealer

Modeling paste layer

INSTRUCTIONS

Preparation

1 Read Basic Techniques, pages 4-7.

2 Create a broken edge on the bottom of the 6" x 8" block. (See Special Techniques, page 8.)

3 Using ½" styrofoam, cut a 1" wide "L"-shaped piece, with one arm 6" in length and the other arm 7½" (see photos).

4 Using ½" styrofoam, cut two strips: ¼" x ¼" x 5¾" and ¼" x ¼" x 4½".

5 Attach the "L"-shaped piece to the top right corner on the front of the block. Break off the end on the bottom to match the broken edge (see photo).

6 Attach the two ¼" strips in place about ¼" from the "L" shaped border. Position the 4½" piece at the top and the 5¾" piece on the right front. Break off the bottom edge of the side strip to match the broken edge of the 6" x 8" block (see photo).

7 Break off one petal from the foam flower. Press the broken edge of the flower onto a hard surface to give a flat edge (see photo).

8 Place a hole for hanging in the back of the block approximately 1" from the top.

9 Papier-mâché the entire block, fitting the papier-mâché carefully around the added styrofoam shapes.

Modeling and Painting

1 Coat the entire block with a layer of modeling paste. Let dry, then texture the top and right side of the block.

2 Using modeling paste, adhere the flower to the front of the block, aligning the flat side with the left side of the block. Place leaves around the flower (see photo for placement and figure a).

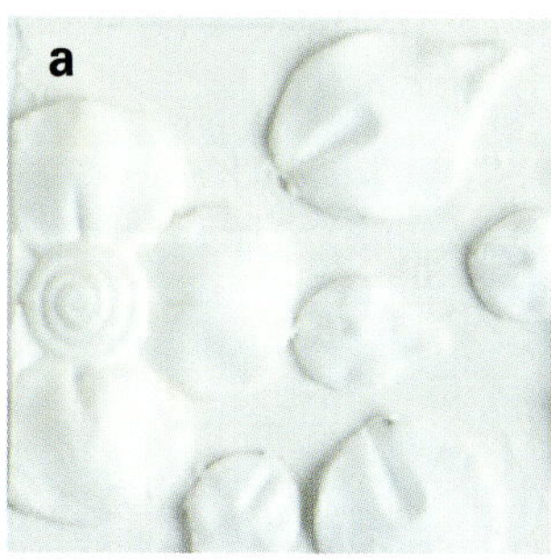

a Adhere foam flower and leaves.

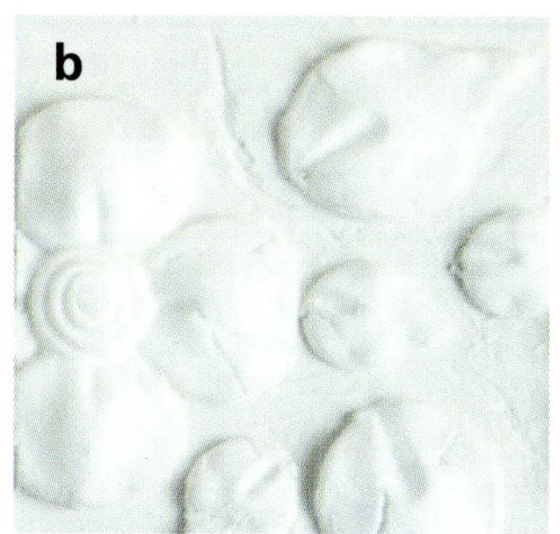

b Create cracks.

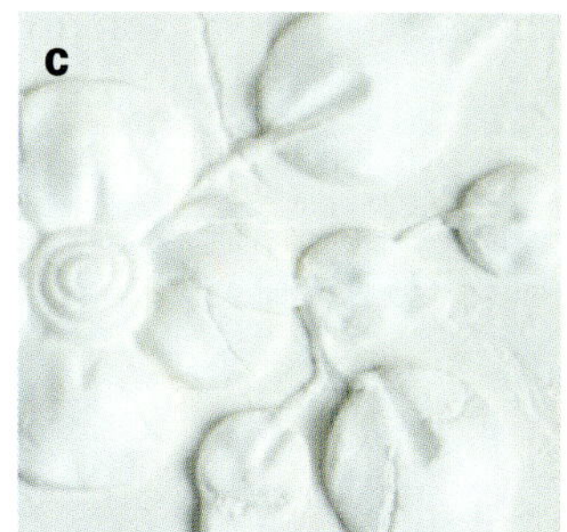

c Use modeling paste to make stems.

3 Create cracks using a serrated knife (see photo for placement and fig b.) (See Special Techniques, page 8.)

4 Make the stems: Thin some modeling paste with water (about one part water to three parts paste). Pick up the mixture with the tip of the brush and drop and pull the mixture along to create stems (see figure c). Correct and shape using a wet cotton swab. Let dry.

5 Basecoat the back of the block with Lamp Black.

6 Basecoat the front and sides with Lt. Buttermilk, including the flowers, stems, and leaves (see figure d).

7 Brush on Soft Black on the sides of the block, between the borders and into the cracks. Use a soft cloth to wipe off, allowing some color to remain, particularly in the crevices.

8 Apply crackle medium around the flower, stems, and leaves, following manufacturer's instructions.

9 Brush on and wipe off Golden Halo and Shadow Tan, allowing color to remain in the crevices and in crackled areas (see figure e). Brush on and wipe off Earth Brown in some areas for darker contrast (see figure f).

10 On the sides of the block, randomly brush on and wipe off Golden Halo, Shadow Tan, Earth Brown, and Soft Black until a weathered effect is achieved. Finish the sides by randomly sponging on Glorious Gold (see photo).

Finishing

1 When thoroughly dry, seal with multi-purpose sealer.

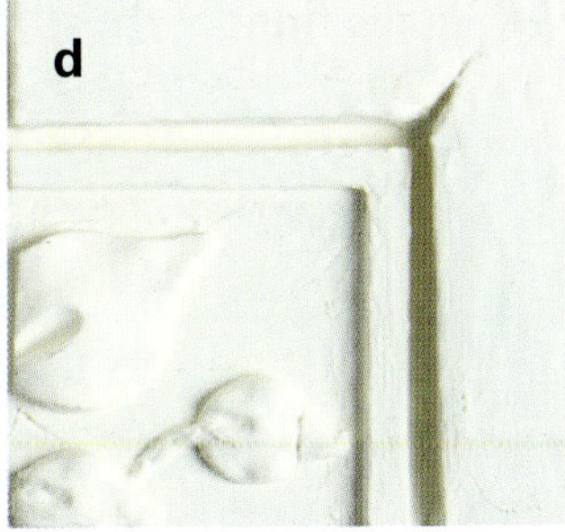

Basecoat Lt. Buttermilk.

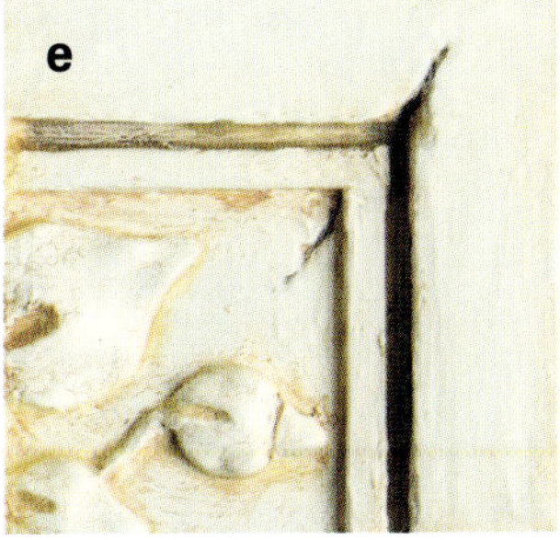

Antique crackle area with Golden Halo and Shadow Tan. Antique cracks with Soft Black.

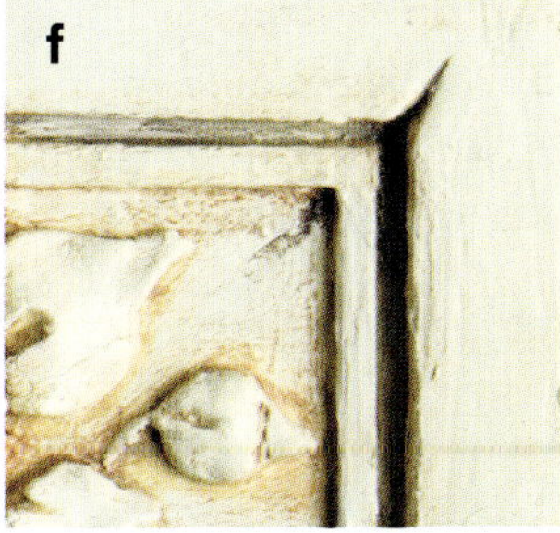

Antique Earth Brown.

WISHES OF LOVE & LUCK

Love is an energy which exists of itself. It is its own value.
—Thornton Wilder

MATERIALS

SURFACE

½" styrofoam, 12" x 24"

PAINTS

DecoArt Americana Acrylics
Lamp Black
Lt. Buttermilk
DecoArt Heavenly Hues
Earth Brown
Golden Halo
Hunter Green
Shadow Tan
DecoArt Dazzling Metallics
Glorious Gold

BRUSHES

Loew Cornell, Inc.
½" and 1" wash/glaze: *Series 7550*
#6 round: *Series 7000*

SUPPLIES

Chinese love/luck symbols stencil *by Plaid Simply Stencil #28234*
Liquitex Modeling Paste
Liquitex Matte Gel Medium
Tacky glue
Soft cloth or paper towels
Stencil sponges or makeup sponges
Cotton swabs
Sandpaper (medium and fine)
DecoArt Multi-Purpose Sealer

INSTRUCTIONS

Preparation

1 Read Basic Techniques, pages 4-7.

2 Cut two 6" x 11¾" pieces of ½" styrofoam. Create a hanging hole in one of the pieces by cutting out a 1" circle approximately 1½" down from the center top. Since this will be the base piece, the hole can penetrate entirely through the ½" styrofoam. Set aside.

3 Trace the pattern for the "broken stone pieces" on page 28 onto tracing paper. Transfer to the other 6" x 11¾" styrofoam piece. Cut the pieces using a serrated knife.

4 Cut two rectangles from ½" styrofoam, measuring 3¼" x 4". Compress the edges of these pieces with your fingers, creating an uneven edge. (See photo.)

5 Papier-mâché all pieces individually.

Modeling and Painting

1 Coat all pieces with a layer of modeling paste.

2 When dry, place the broken pieces over the bottom piece and trace along the broken edges to assist in placing the stenciled words "love" and "luck". Remove broken pieces.

3 Place the stencil for "love" and "luck" on the block and trace the words in order to check placement.

愛
love
幸
luck

When satisfied with their position, apply the stenciled design using modeling paste. (See Special Techniques, page 10.)

4 Use the same method to place the characters for love and luck on the two small rectangular blocks, using modeling paste to apply the design. When these stenciled areas are thoroughly dry, sand gently with medium sandpaper to smooth. Finish with fine sandpaper, making sure the stenciled areas are flat and smooth.

5 Basecoat all pieces with Light Buttermilk.

6 Brush on Golden Halo on the "broken pieces" and wipe off with a soft cloth (see figure a). Repeat with Hunter Green (see figure b). Repeat with Earth Brown (see figure c). Allow the predominant color to be Hunter Green (see photo).

7 Brush on Golden Halo and Shadow Tan on all sides of the 6" x 11 ¾" block and wipe off, allowing more color to remain around the stenciled letters.

8 Brush on Golden Halo and Shadow Tan on the front and sides of pieces stenciled with Chinese characters, and wipe off, allowing more Shadow Tan to remain around stenciled areas (see figure e).

9 Dip a sponge in Glorious Gold, blot and sponge lightly around the front and side edges of the small blocks (see figure f).

10 Place the stencil for the "love" character over its raised stencil. Dip a sponge into Lamp Black and blot well on a paper towel. Gently sponge Lamp Black over the stenciled area. Remove the stencil. Repeat for the "luck" character.

11 Glue "broken" pieces in place over the base block, using tacky glue. Glue small blocks in place with tacky glue, checking carefully that the correct character is placed over the corresponding word.

Finishing

1 When thoroughly dry, seal the entire piece with multi-purpose sealer.

Modeling paste layer

Basecoat Lt. Buttermilk. Antique Golden Halo.

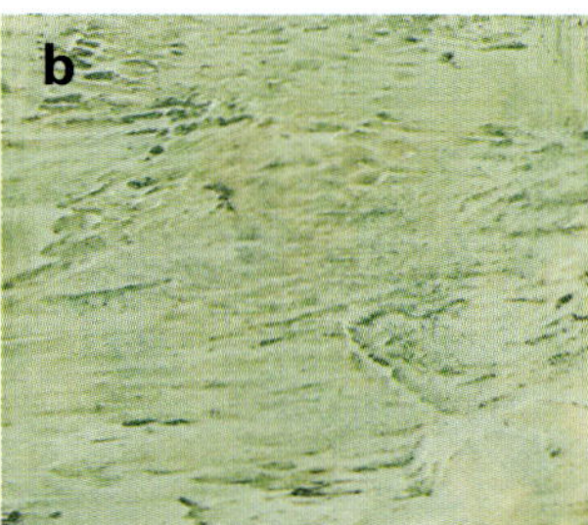

Antique Hunter Green.

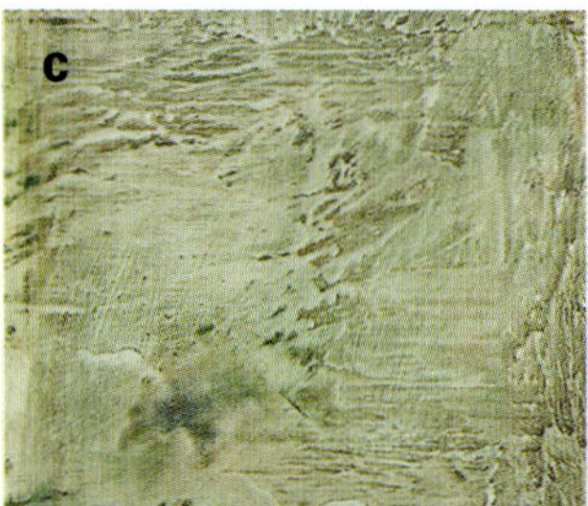

Antique Earth Brown. Allow the Hunter Green to predominate.

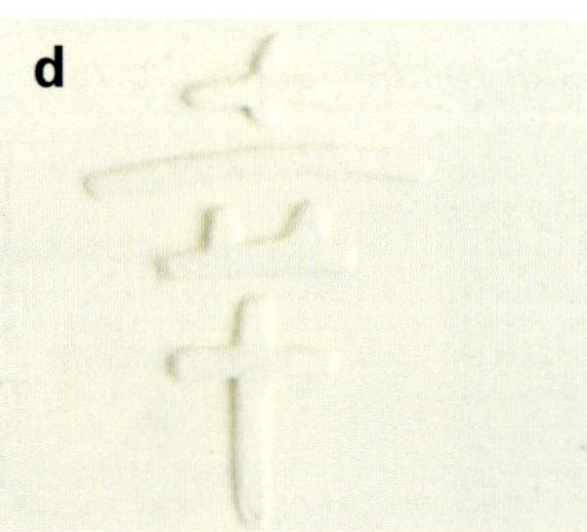

Basecoat Lt. Buttermilk.

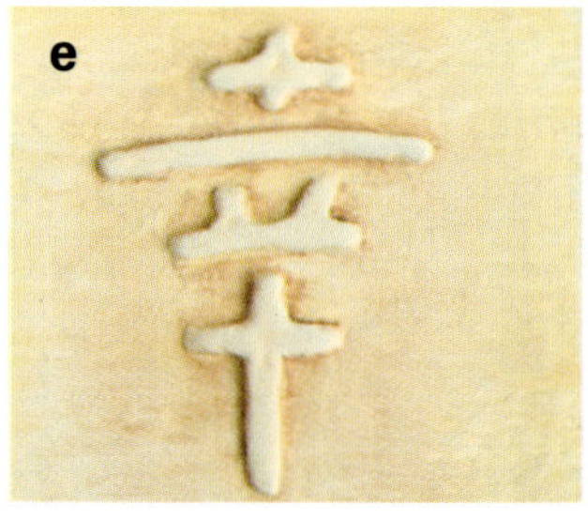

Antique Golden Halo and Shadow Tan.

Randomly and lightly sponge Glorious Gold around edges. Paint stencil characters Lamp Black.

SOURCES

The products used to create the designs in this book are available at your local craft retailer. For specialty items or assistance in locating a retailer, consult the companies below.

BYRDWELL CREATIONS
Acrylic paint conversion charts
Betty L. Byrd's Acrylic Conversions
1513 Commanche Drive
Las Vegas, NV 89109
702-735-7065
http://www.4dbyrds.com
bettybyrd@4dbyrds.com

CHEAP JOE'S ART STUFF
Modeling paste, matte gel medium
374 Industrial Park Drive
Boone, NC 28607
800-227-2788
www.cheapjoes.com

DECOART
Acrylic paints, crackle medium
P.O. Box 386
Stanford, KY 40484
800-367-3047
www.decoart.com

DELTA TECHNICAL COATINGS
Renaissance Foil Easy Gold Leafing System
2550 Pelissier Place
Whittier, CA 90601
800-423-4135
www.deltacrafts.com

DESIGN A LINE, INC.
KREATIVE FOAM
Foam shapes and ornaments
Saratoga Springs, Utah 84043
www.kreativefoam.com

FLORACRAFT CORPORATION
STYROFOAM* BRAND FOAM
Styrofoam and Wonder Cutter *cutting tool*
P.O. Box 400
Ludington, MI 49431
postmaster@floracraft.com
www.floracraft.com

JUMA FARMS, LTD.
Wood letters
3165 Highway 594
Monroe, LA 71203
318-345-1500

LIQUITEX ARTIST MATERIALS
Modeling paste, matte gel medium
P.O. Box 246
Piscataway, NJ 08855
800-445-4278
www.liquitex.com

LOEW-CORNELL, INC.
Brushes
563 Chestnut Avenue
Teaneck, NJ 07666
201-836-7070
loew-cornell@loew-cornell.com
www.loewcornell.com

MILESTONES
Stone stamps
15127 NE 24th Street, #332
Redmond, WA 98052-5547
www.milestonescrafts.com

MOSAIC MERCANTILE
Mosaic tiles
P.O. Box 78206
San Francisco, CA 94107
877-9-MOSAIC
E-mail:
MOSAIC@MOSAICMERC.COM
www.mosaicmerc.com

PLAID ENTERPRISES, INC.
Stencils, Faster Plaster, reusable molds
P.O. Box 7600
Norcross, GA 30091-7600
770-923-8200
www.plaidonline.com

WALNUT HOLLOW
Classic Dimensions Decorative Wood Pieces
1409 State Road 23
Dodgeville, WI 53533
800-950-5101
www.walnuthollow.com

*Trademark of The Dow Chemical Co.

Acrylic Paint Conversions

DecoArt Americana	*Delta Ceramcoat*	*Plaid FolkArt*
Black Green	Black Green	Wrought Iron
Burnt Umber	Burnt Umber	Burnt Umber
Buttermilk	Antique White	Tapioca, Warm White
Desert Turquoise	Colonial Blue	Aqua + Cerulean Blue/AP
Green Mist	Oasis Green	Poetry Green
Lamp Black	Black	Licorice
Light Buttermilk	Light Ivory	Ivory White
Pansy Lavender	Vintage Wine + White	Diox. Purple + Plum Pudding
Payne's Grey	Midnight Blue, Blue Storm	Payne's Grey
Rookwood Red	Candy Bar Brown, Cinnamon	Apple Spice
Soft Peach	White + Pumpkin	White + Glazed Carrots
Taupe	Taupe	Potpourri Rose + Dk. Gray + W.
Violet Haze	Purple Dusk	Periwinkle
Wisteria	Bahama Purple + Lisa Pink + White	Heather + Coastline Blue + W.

Dazzling Metallics	*Gleams*	*Metallics*
Bronze	Copper	Copper
Copper	Red Copper	Copper
Glorious Gold	Kim Gold	Pure Gold
Royal Ruby	Red Copper	Regal Red + Amethyst
Shimmering Silver	Metallic Silver	Silver Sterling
Venetian Gold	Kim Gold	Antique Gold

If Heavenly Hues paints are not available at your local craft store, you can achieve a similar effect by mixing the following acrylics with DecoArt Staining/Antiquing Medium:

Heavenly Hues	*DecoArt Americana*
Angel Flesh	Hi-Lite Flesh
Earth Brown	Sable Brown
Golden Halo	French Vanilla
Hunter Green	Forest Green (closest)
Patina Green	Mint Julep (not exact)
Purple Heather	Wild Orchid (lighter) or Lavender (darker)
Sea Spray	Indian Turquoise (closest)
Shadow Tan	Mink Tan
Soft Black	Graphite
Terra Cotta	Shading Flesh (lighter) or Dark Flesh (darker)

KEY: comma = separates two color choices
White or W. = white of choice
+ = mix two colors together

Heavenly Hues conversions provided by DecoArt. All other conversions are from Betty L. Byrd's Acrylic Conversions - 7th Edition, *which contains complete charts for eight leading brands of acrylic paints. Books are available at your local craft store or contact Byrdwell Creations – KDS, 1513 Commanche Dr., Las Vegas, NV 89109. http://www.4dbyrds.com; email: bettybyrd@4dbyrds.com (no phone orders.)*